To len & Lyn

GIBBO

Best wishes,

David Gibson

Leicester City F.C

GIBBO

THE DAVIE GIBSON STORY

with CHRIS WESTCOTT

AMBERLEY

I would like to dedicate this book to my wife Mavis, my family and to all the friends I met along the way.

First published 2013

Amberley Publishing
The Hill, Stroud
Gloucestershire, GL5 4EP

www.amberley-books.com

British Library Cataloguing in Publication Data.
A catalogue record for this book is available from the British Library.

ISBN 978 1 4456 1354 3
E-book ISBN 978 1 4456 1361 1

Typeset in 10pt on 12pt Sabon.
Typesetting and Origination by Amberley Publishing.
Printed in the UK.

Contents

Introduction

It's Saturday 25 May 1963 and I'm at Wembley Stadium, the most famous football stadium in the world, even for a Scot. To be precise, I'm not just at Wembley: deep beneath those iconic Twin Towers I'm anxiously perched on the wooden bench in the dressing room with my Leicester City team-mates, awaiting the call to line up in the tunnel. A little over an hour earlier we had been gently driven by coach along Wembley Way, surrounded by thousands of fans making their way to the venue of the highlight of the season, the FA Cup final. Sporting blue and white rosettes and scarves, the City fans shout, cheer and wave as we pass by. Among them we spot the red of the opposition supporters, Manchester United, and they jeer and boo, good-natured banter I hope.

There's quite a buzz in our dressing room. I've read the pen pictures of all the players in the programme – 'Brilliant, bow-legged Scot. A really talented ball player, accurate forward general of the side, switches play with baffling speed. Modest, likeable young man.' I'm happy with that! The jersey and pants are neatly laid out. A few players are quietly going through their match-day ritual – examining boots, making sure the studs are screwed in tight, then checking their laces are the correct length.

I look around and there's our captain Colin Appleton, whose greatest wish is to climb the thirty-nine steps in a couple of hours to meet the Queen and lift the Cup above his head. We all hope for that. Colin's striding around the room wishing everyone all the best. I glance towards Frank McLintock, my great friend who I call 'D'Artagnan'. He's a musketeer, a fighter, a winner and a wonderful player to have on your side. He was here two years ago when the Foxes lost to the superb Tottenham side that won the League and Cup 'double'. Frank won't contemplate losing again.

Every few minutes someone heads to the toilet, maybe for a last drag on a fag or a sly tipple. Or maybe their anxiety demands an emergency visit. There's Banksie, the great Gordon Banks, a future World Cup winner. He's fiddling with a football, bouncing it against a wall and catching it. Again and again and again – could it be nerves? Never, Banksie was too experienced to be nervous, or was he? Nerves? Yes, of course on all match days, but even more so on a huge occasion like today. The outcome of the match will depend on how we handle that anxiety. Once the referee blows the whistle

I'm sure the nerves will disperse and all will be fine. I finally pull on my kit – shorts, socks and new jersey with number 10 stitched onto the back. To any young readers, I was an inside left, now termed a left-sided midfield player. I think back to a boyhood hero, Hollywood star James Cagney, who in the film *White Heat* said, 'Made it Ma, top of the world.' That's how I feel in that Wembley dressing room. Could my life as a footballer get any better or happier? I'm on top of the world, about to venture along that long tunnel and onto the field of my dreams, the lush turf that I've dreamt of playing on since I was a wee lad.

Suddenly the patient wait is over – we're called to leave the dressing room and line up in the tunnel with the opposition. Matt Gillies heads the team alongside Matt Busby, two proud Scottish managers leading their sides out to contest the most famous of all club knock-out competitions. On the United side I glance at Paddy Crerand – as kids with Hibernian and Celtic, we faced each other. As for Denis Law, I've seen more fat on a chip but on his day he can roast any defence. We exchange brief formalities, words of greeting, 'Hi Paddy, good luck' and 'Hello Denis' and nod heads in appreciation of the moment.

We start the long walk, we're on our way and what an emotional walk it is. Every young boy ought to have the opportunity to embrace the feeling of emerging into this wonderful stadium for the first time. To appreciate it, to savour the moment, it's almost impossible to describe the emotion. Near the mouth of the tunnel I can just see the blue sky peeping out. The hairs on the back of my neck stand up as the fans opposite catch a glimpse of us emerging. The crowd explodes, a sea of blue, red and white, clapping and cheering. We stride out purposefully onto that magnificent carpet of grass and are introduced to the Duke of Edinburgh.

This is the moment I've been waiting for, appearing at Wembley in the FA Cup final. That may seem a strange ambition for a Scot. Should it not be Hampden Park or playing for Scotland? The truth is that, from the day Stanley Matthews turned on his magic in the 1953 Cup final, I've been captivated by the romance and glamour of a Wembley final. The thrilling finish when he fully earned his winner's medal inspired in me a dream. Exactly ten years on from that memorable match in the year of Queen Elizabeth's Coronation, here I am fulfilling my boyhood ambition.

How did a wee lad, shy and insecure, manage to bridge that divide between Winchburgh and Wembley – where did it all start? I'm getting ahead of myself, my Voyage of Dreams...

I

The Miners' Rows

Shale mining has a lengthy history in West Lothian. James 'Paraffin' Young patented a method for producing oil from coal and shale in the mid-nineteenth century. It was big business; in 1913 the West Lothian output of crude oil peaked at over 17 million barrels. Oil imported from overseas gradually made the local production uneconomic but, while the industry finally ceased in the 1960s, it was still a major economy when I was born at home on 23 September 1938 in the small mining village of Winchburgh, about 10 miles west of Edinburgh. While my father David wasn't actually a miner, he worked at the local works, which mined the shale and extracted oil from it. He was based in the sulphur house, sulphur being one of the properties of shale oil.

Home was 58 Abercorn Place, one of many houses in the miners' rows. These early houses were generally built in rows to save materials and space, and huddled together near collieries. Mum, whose name was Isabella or Isa for short, dad and my sister Mary all lived in the front room of the Haddows' family house, sharing the kitchen and outside toilets with Mrs Haddow and her kids. Shortly after I was born we were given our own one-bedroom corner house in the new rows at 113 Craigton Place. Later we swapped with the O'Haras, who lived next door at 114, once their family had grown up and moved out, so that my sister could have her own bedroom. Within the living room was a table, a fireplace and a recess built in between three walls, where mum and dad slept. We had a gas mantle for lighting, a crystal set receiver, later known as a wireless, but definitely no central heating. I wouldn't venture out of bed until mum made the fire, knelt down and warmed my clothes. Out I would come from under the blankets that kept me warm during the night.

My favourite meal as a kid was minced beef and mashed potatoes, otherwise known as mince and tatties. Dad had an allotment so if we were lucky it may have been supplemented with some peas. At the weekend there might be ham and eggs, but no great delicacies. If you had custard, it would be with rhubarb from the allotment. The Gibson family was on the short side, my dad, mum, Mary and naturally me. Dad was 5 foot nothing of pure gold and when mum placed my food in front of me she'd say, 'Eat your dinner up and you'll be a big man like Mr O'Hara next door' – he was a 6-foot giant. Happy days for me but difficult for mum, with wartime ration books and stamps you used at the local Co-op to purchase the groceries.

A watercolour of the Miners' Rows at Winchburgh, with our local football field in the foreground. Our corner house in Craigton Place is on the right, with the car parked in front.

There was no history of anyone in the family playing any sport – I must have been a freak. Perhaps it was destiny, but the front of the house looked onto the local fitba field and one of Scotland's finest footballers, Willie Thornton, centre-forward of Glasgow Rangers, lived a few doors away. As kids could we ever forget those Sunday afternoons when our football match would stop, just to shout 'Hi' to Willie and his footballing colleagues like Willie Waddell and Torry Gillick, who were visiting for afternoon tea? It really made our day just to hear our hero say, 'Hello boys.' Over the years this little village has produced its fair share of footballers who made it to the professional ranks: goalkeeper Bill Harper of Hibs, Arsenal and Plymouth Argyle; Jimmy McLean of Hibs and Stirling Albion; Ross Menzies of Rangers; another keeper, Willie Duff of Hearts, Charlton and Peterborough; and John Gorman of Celtic, Carlisle and Spurs, all of whom started out on the recreation park at Winchburgh. This football field would be my second home for the next fifteen years, my favourite playground. With the rest of the gang we'd play and dream we were Stanley Matthews, Billy Steel, Gordon Smith or my boyhood hero Willie Bauld.

Of course war broke out within a year of my birth. I've always been blessed with a decent memory and must have been just four years old when the siren went off at the local oil works as German aircraft approached to drop their incendiary bombs. I remember being awakened and carried to the air-raid shelter, constructed at the foot of Tongue Hill, the other end of the football field. It housed about five families; that same hill where in the years to come we'd play Cowboys and Indians all summer before it became our winter Olympics venue. Davie Menzies was the king of the hill, he had the most modern of toboggans. The rest of us made do with bits of wood nailed together or an old bathtub or tea tray, a far cry from the modern contraptions, but we loved it just the same.

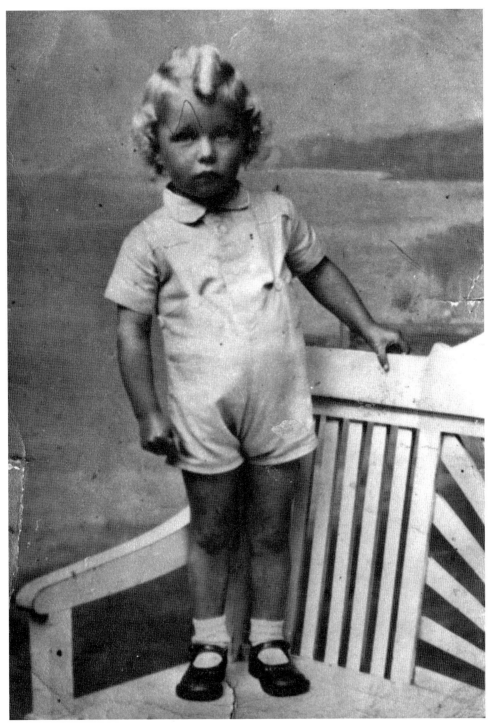

A bonny wee young two-year-old – where did all the hair go?

Winchburgh Primary School class photo, 1946. I'm in the front row, extreme left.

At five years old, it was time for my first day at Winchburgh Primary School. My only memory of that special morning was a girl called Jean Mackie who cried her eyes out when her mum left her at the school gates. I do remember the second day when mum woke me up and said, 'School time David.' 'I went yesterday,' I replied. I thought that was it.

I'm afraid I wasn't the most enthusiastic of scholars in the class. As Miss Miller, one of the teachers, said, 'Gibson, your brains are in your feet.' If I experienced any problems in the maths department my pal Roy Rutherford helped me out. Roy should have been the Chancellor of the Exchequer – he was brilliant. I only won one award in all my years at school, that of Sportsman of the Year in 1953, presented by Mr Green, the headmaster of the local Catholic school. My present was a book on the Kon-Tiki expedition. I've never forgotten it or Mr Green. A year prior to that presentation I had been playing on my own in his school playground, kicking the ball against the wall. When it rebounded I volleyed it with my other foot against the opposite wall, all good practice. All went well for a while until 'Crash', my volley went straight through Mr Green's window. Panic set in as I climbed over the far wall and ran practically all round the village to get home, which was actually only 50 yards away. However, I couldn't live with my guilt and plucked up the courage to make my way to Mr Green's house. 'I'm very sorry but I've just broken your school window, playing football in the play-ground,' I uttered anxiously. To my immense relief he smiled and appreciated my honesty. To this day I am convinced that gesture won me the award. I met him subsequently over the years and learnt to appreciate he was a genuinely nice man.

I couldn't wait for the bell to ring then dashed outside to the playground. The Catholic school had the best five-a-side playground in the village – many a time the gang were chased out of it. When we caught sight of Jimmy Mackie, the local copper, riding his bike towards the school, 'Scatter' was the call we used to avoid trouble.

2

Wee Tanner Ba

My best pal for nigh-on ten years was a wee tanner ba. For the price of a tanner or sixpence, the ba or ball was made of cheap rubber that only measured about six inches in diameter. It could be found in Scotland as early as the 1920s but gained in popularity in the lean years following the war.

I am indebted to my pal Billy Hunter who, after a successful career with Motherwell and Scotland, reinvented himself as a published poet. This marvellous poem illustrates the point:

> Ah well I remember the day, when I was just a lad at play
> And fitba games I did nae give a straw,
> My father said 'Hey son throw away that silly gun,
> You can have a lot more fun with a wee tanner ba.'
> He taught me how to shoot, how to trap it with my boot,
> How to tame it when it tried to run awa.
> I was nae daft, I was nae glacket, when a goal I had to take it,
> Between my jersey and my jacket went the wee tanner ba.
> When the school I left behind, and a job I had to find,
> A football scout said 'What's your name an awe?'
> 'It's Willie Brown,' I said with pride, 'And I'll play for your side,
> As long as you provide a wee tanner ba.'
> Well for Scotland I was capped, how they thundered and they clapped.
> 'Cos I played a game without a flaw,
> The goalie started praying,
> 'Cos I dreamed I was playing with my wee tanner ba.
> It was at Hampden Park, the Queen was heard to remark,
> 'Wha's that laddie, where did he learn to play the game so braw?'
> If your majesty must know I learnt it long ago,
> With my wee tanner ba.
> So all you wishful daddies, when you're bringing up your laddies,
> You can make them play as well as Denis Law.

Think of that colossal pay, for such a small outlay, if you start them off the day,
With the wee tanner ba.

Sandy Scott was the best dribbler in the playground and Sandy was a wee tubby guy – who needed pace when you could dribble like Sandy? This was where I was happiest, with a ball at my feet. When mum asked me to run to the shops for the groceries, out came the tanner ba and I dribbled round grannies and grandads all the way to the shops and back. It taught me great ball control, although of course I didn't appreciate it at the time.

Real footballs were hard to come by because of the cost and brand-new balls only came around at Christmas time. Old balls were repaired if someone in the gang had a good outside and somebody else an inside, i.e. the bladder. The gang saved up for months after we spotted a new football in a shop near Tynecastle. One Saturday afternoon we made our way to watch Hearts play in Edinburgh. The ball was still in the window and we planned to buy it for about 25 shillings after the game. However, we were nervous, as in our naivety we thought it was the only one in the shop. In anticipation of kicking a new ball we couldn't wait for the final whistle and left at half-time to buy it. We all took turns in holding the ball on the bus home – next stop the fitba field. Who needed Wembley when we had our own paradise? We enjoyed many happy days and five-a-side competitions fought out with that bargain.

I have several wonderful memories of growing up in Winchburgh, including the morning and evening paper rounds I did for the post office. The morning round was along the main street, finishing at the school playground. If I were running a little behind, the gang would come out of the playground and deliver a paper each, so I wouldn't be late for the first lesson. Fridays were always the hardest as, in addition to the daily papers, you had to carry the *Weekly News*, the *Radio Times* and the local *Courier* – all that for six bob a week (30p in today's money). The other round was the Sunday morning newspapers for another 6 shillings. As the shops were closed on a Sunday I started at Wattie Reid's house. He was one of the charge-hands who worked with my dad and lived in the miners' rows. I would leave Wattie's house between 7.30 and 8 o'clock and my first delivery was to Curly Paterson, the *Sunday Post* and the *People* for 5 pence. Mrs Paterson would invite me in for a huge breakfast of bacon and eggs, fried bread, toast and tea. By the time I finished, her husband and son had read all the other papers in my bag, which I thought was fair exchange. The number of times old Wattie wandered around trying to find me when my customers complained I was over an hour late with their Sunday paper. He never did find me tucking into my fry-up at Mrs Paterson's. On top of that was the store or Co-op run, cycling on Saturdays to the shops to pick up the groceries for my auntie Annie and auntie May and collecting my grandad's pension. That was worth another six bob for me – I thought I was a millionaire at fifteen!

Another chance to earn some more cash was the village Gala Day, with the crowning of the queen, a five-a-side competition and races. Not that I was very quick, but I knew someone who was. Ishbelle Wishart was seriously rapid, so I asked if she would partner me in the thread the needle race. She would run the first leg with the needle and I waited at the other end of the field with the thread. All I had to do was thread the needle, then run back with her to the winning post. I was pretty good at threading the needle for my mother at home and Ishbelle did her bit – she gave me about three seconds' start on the rest of the field. Sadly, in the excitement my eyes and nerves let me down. Ishbelle was still standing beside me laughing as the next race was due to start.

The years went whizzing past – as kids we were into everything – if it was out of bounds we were there. Material objects didn't matter to us – as long as we could swim in the canal, steal apples from the orchards or fish in the local burn, we were very happy. The Glasgow–Edinburgh railway line practically ran through our village. Just after the war, when the soldiers were demobbed and returning home, the gang was forever down on the track scrounging for anything that had been thrown out of the train. Tins of corned beef or American chewing gum were two of the many items we found on the line. We never realised how dangerous it was standing so close, with trains flashing past at terrific speed.

In the village there were parties in the street to celebrate the end of the conflict. Soldiers returning from the front reverted to dads, surely the future was going to be better. As kids and families, everyone was in the same position – poor – but nobody felt inferior. Families helped each other and looking back, while of course we have gained hugely in material wealth, has it been to the detriment of the camaraderie that used to exist with your next-door neighbour?

Television was in its infancy – nobody in the road had one until our neighbour Mrs Parker, whose daughter worked in the electrical shop at Broxburn, purchased one of the first TVs in the village. It had a magnificent magnifying screen to enlarge the picture. The Matthews Cup final against Bolton Wanderers in May 1953 was the first time I saw a match on television. All the kids were jammed in the sitting room, fascinated by this master of the dribble. In one of the most exciting finishes of all Cup finals, Stanley Matthews produced sheer magic in the final twenty minutes as Blackpool recovered from a 3-1 deficit. In virtually the last minute Stan Mortensen equalised by completing the last hat-trick scored in an FA Cup final. By the time Bill Perry followed up with the winner in injury time, I'd seen enough to decide what I wanted to be when I grew up. This match was followed on television by England's defeat to Hungary in November 1953. At fifteen years old I realised they were playing a completely different game. The Magical Magyars, led by Ferenc Puskás, a small tubby genius, completely transformed my ideas of how football should be played. Their possession, passing and movement was so easy on the eye, such entertainment, and a joy to watch. It was so good I asked Mrs Parker if I could came back and watch the highlights at night-time!

Every Friday afternoon the fruit man arrived at the rows. One of the gang waited until he was busy with a customer, moved to the other side of his wagon where he couldn't see us and pinched an orange or an apple. One day it was my turn. The wee man as we called him was busy serving Mrs Greaves, the biggest and loudest old lady in the rows. I crept to the other side, took my apple and slipped away unseen. Easy if you haven't a conscience but mine took over and told me to put it back. I eased my way back to the wagon and placed the apple gently on the rear of the lorry, which had been released to hold the potato bags. Unfortunately, the apple ran down between the bags

)ad. The wee man and Mrs Greaves still hadn't spotted anything untoward,
; I was picking up the apple to put it back, my luck ran out. Mrs Greaves
und and bellowed, 'What the hell are you playing at, caught you red handed.'
vould have it my mum was outside brushing the carpet about 50 yards away.
She heard Mrs Greaves' voice; 'What's that?' she called out. 'He's stealing apples Isa.'
I'm certain the whole of the rows heard her. My mum must have hit me with every
yard of her long handle brush. Today she would be arrested for assault and battery.
'Just wait until your father comes home and you will get another one,' she shouted to
add insult to injury. In those days you were hit with whatever object your mother was
holding to save her precious hands from being injured. Many years later I mentioned
at mum and dad's golden wedding anniversary that we were lucky they were still with
us and not in jail for that assault!

Another assault occurred when I had a 'paddy' under the table, screaming, shouting
and banging my feet. Mum put up with this tantrum for a couple of minutes when she
let fly with the first thing in her hand. Unfortunately for me it was a pair of scissors.
She aimed well or perhaps I was unlucky, as the scissors stuck in my leg and there was
blood everywhere. 'You've killed me,' I shouted. Mum wasn't overly sympathetic. 'If
I catch you I'll definitely bloody well kill you.' Looking back, I'm certain all the kids
were treated the same and hopefully we became better people for it.

Summer holidays were spent at the house of auntie Anne, uncle Jim and grandad in
Millgate and I loved every minute of it. Aged eight, with my suitcase packed, off I went
just over the canal bridge roughly 500 yards away. They lived in a new house built
after the war and it felt like paradise. To say I was spoilt would be an understatement.
Whenever I wanted something, a sweetie, an apple or a penny, I only had to ask. I also
picked up my first nickname there. Uncle Jimmy was a sergeant in the Army, 6 feet tall
and to a kid about 4 feet nothing and weighing 3 stone he was enormous. One day
when I was soaking wet he shouted to me, 'Hey skin', and it stuck.

Grandad had hens in the back garden, he and his brother loved to lock me in with the
cockerel and killed themselves with laughter, as I shit myself with fright. The six weeks'
holiday always passed quickly and when it was time to return home I'd climb under
the bed and hold onto the mattress springs. 'I don't want to go home,' I shouted at my
dad when he tried to untangle me from the springs. The laughs and happy memories I
had in those few years will live with me forever.

When grandad died a few years later, all the relatives came back to the house. My
cousin and I were lying in front of the fireplace beside this old man, who was sitting
in grandad's chair. We found out later his name was Sam Ravie – he must have been
about 100 and certainly looked that old to us. As we lay in front of him we couldn't
help but notice an enormous lump on his forehead. I plucked up the courage to ask
him, 'Mister what's that lump on your head?' He must have been asked dozens of times
and explained that he used to be a blacksmith in the local works. The man working
beside him was his chapper Charlie, whose tool of trade was a big hammer. When Sam
wanted him to shape the metal, he would tap the spot he wanted Charlie to hit and
told him, 'When I nod my head, hit it!' It took us a long time to work out that old Sam
had kidded us on.

Football was of course our passion every day of the week, even on the day of rest. Sunday was the one time you dressed up – a new suit, shirt, tie and shoes for Sunday school. The problem was that most of the guys had only one pair of shoes and you had to keep them spotless. The last words my mum spoke to me before I left for church were, 'Keep yourself clean, no football in those new shoes after church.' In my excitement to reach the football field mum's words were always quickly forgotten, jackets were flung off for goalposts and the game started. One hour later all the mums in the rows shouted out our names; 'Dinner's ready.' Panic set in as our shirts were sticking out of our trousers, ties were all askew and we were sweating buckets. We could fix the shirt and ties, but what about the shoes? Jimmy Wilson, one of the gang, came up with the solution – pull up a handful of grass and use it to wipe the mud off his shoes. To a point it worked, all our shoes looked clean if not spotless and we survived until the following Sunday.

Between the football, swimming in the canal or stealing apples, we'd visit the local picture house at Broxburn. We had just enough money to get in, plus a black pudding supper shared between four of us on the long 2½-mile walk home, as we couldn't afford the bus fare as well. The film showing one day was *The Harlem Globetrotters*. Up to then we never knew what basketball was. They were magicians with the ball and their brilliant theme tune was 'Sweet Georgia Brown'. We loved it so much we hid under the seats until the second performance to see it again. Goose Tatum was one of their stars and a great showman.

Jimmy Mackie was public enemy number one, well he was to us. Every morning when I left the house mum's last words were always, 'Don't let the policeman bring you home.' On Sunday afternoons after football the gang played in the canal boat, which was naturally out of bounds. We managed to untie its moorings one day and sailed off down the canal in 'Tom Sawyer' or 'Huckleberry Finn' fashion, but became stuck at the very first of the canal bridges. As we couldn't move the boat back to its moorings we had to leave it there. Arriving home, mum asked, 'Where have you been playing today?' 'Cowboys and Indians up the hill.' I'm sure I said that every time I came home.

Next day while playing in the backyard, Jimmy stopped and asked if we were on the canal boat yesterday. 'Not me,' I replied – wrong answer! He went on his way to find another member of the gang. My mum witnessed it all and asked what Jimmy wanted. I had of course already told her I wasn't on the boat. Later that night, crossing the football field, who else but Jimmy Mackie shone his torch on me. 'Come here, you told me you weren't on the canal boat yesterday and you lied. Get yourself home now and tell your mother I'll be along in a minute.' I was still standing at the front door, too frightened to tell my mum, when Jimmy arrived. 'Mrs Gibson, your son was playing on the canal boat with the rest of his cronies.' Now I was in big trouble, one for lying and two for being on the canal. Fortunately mum's sister was visiting and asked the copper if her own son Peter was on the boat too. He was – Jimmy would be along to discuss it later. With that she flew out of the door to have words with Peter. We were all let off with a warning and luckily my mum forgot to belt me when her sister ran out of the house. It was only later when I had children of my own that I could understand mum telling me not to go near the canal. Jimmy was also giving the best advice for our own safety, but when do kids listen?

Follow the Leader was another topper of a game – Tosh Reid was the leader. Whatever he did the gang had to follow, like grabbing a rope and swinging over the burn or stepping over larger stones to cross it. From one side of the brook to the other was a leap of about 6 feet, quite a jump if you were only eight years old. We called the widest part 'Beechers Brook', high on the jumping side down and across to the other. The leader took off – 'Made it – you're not in the gang until you make the jump,' said Tosh. We had two or three attempts before plucking up the courage to take off and land on the other side. Everyone that is but John Syme, who'd just had the plaster removed after breaking his arm. He was finally persuaded to take the jump, but unfortunately fell forward on landing and broke his other arm. We still felt he was a hero for trying but his parents were none too pleased!

The highlight of the summer holiday was the triangular football tournament between the old rows and the new rows (Duntarvie View). The leader of the old rows was George or 'Pidge' Rutherford, brother of my pal Roy and named after his father 'Old Pidge'. Pidge was three years older than us and a real man of the world in our eyes. He was the hero of the old rows gang. He was Bill Struth, Glasgow Rangers manager, he was the mysterious Red Shadow in *The Desert Song* with his flowing coat and whistle, shouting to his gang when he ran off into the wild blue yonder. He was Johnny Weissmuller, Tarzan in the movies, Al Capone when he wanted to be; we were all in awe of him. Pidge was ahead of his time and is still going strong in his seventies. If anyone in his team was playing badly they were put on the transfer list. A fee of 100 chewing gum cards was the going rate for transfers. Pidge transferred Billy Getty for Ann Black once. 'But she's a lassie,' Billy protested. 'I don't care, she's a better player than you.'

When we were about ten years old, the new rows played the old rows in a five-a-side competition for a silver cup, which was designed to be a replica of the Scottish Cup. Mrs Rutherford was a little concerned when Roy asked his mum to buy some silver paint from the post office and make it look like the Scottish Cup. She did go ahead and paint it, and it was worth winning. We (the new rows) beat the old rows but when it came to handing over the cup Roy refused, threw it on the ground and stamped on it, smashing it to pieces. I confronted Mrs Rutherford with what was left of the cup and she told Roy to apologise to our team. He reluctantly did and turned to his mum, 'It's o.k. ma, I know where we can get another one. In the graveyard down in the cemetery.' Roy had sneaked in and stolen a vase from one of the graves. Mrs Rutherford blew a fuse – she thought there was something familiar about that cup as she painted it. Needless to say we never played for another 'Scottish Cup'!

The Rutherfords' father Old Pidge was the green keeper at the local bowling club. We thought the green looked like Wembley – we would watch the old men play bowls while dreaming of playing five-a-side football on that magnificent carpet. We didn't quite play football on it, but one day three of the gang managed to climb over the railings and for a few seconds dreamt we were Stanley Matthews haring down the right wing at Wembley. When I came back home one year from Leicester during the close season my dad, being a bowler, asked me if I fancied a game. I met Old Pidge and, as I didn't have any bowls to play with, he lent me some of his. Not knowing too much about the game I asked how you delivered the bowls. 'Just lay the bowls on the grass,' said Old Pidge, 'and they will sniff their way to the jack.' Now that's what I call coaching.

Next door to the bowling club was Winchburgh Institute, where weddings and special functions were held. It was also the venue for billiards, snooker, dominoes and a reading room for old age pensioners. The only problem was that you had to be over fourteen years old before you could enter the hall. As a kid I often peered through the stained glass window with one eye and saw the three billiard and snooker tables being cleaned and polished by Dick Gibb. He was in charge of the hall on Friday nights, which were called the Flyer Nights. There were billiard competitions in one room and dominoes in another – sixpence to play in each competition. Joe Nugent was the star performer – he was a bit special. The rules were fifty maximum – most of us had handicaps of up to about thirty. Joe was about minus thirty, but he still won most of the competitions. In the other room dominoes was for the more mature men and some old-age pensioners. Old Sam Ravie with the lump on his head had an unusual way of laying down his dominoes – hidden in his hand, he would slide them down onto the table. That was fine until a spectator remarked, 'Hey, someone's played a four against a five.' I wondered how many times Sam got away with it!

One Wednesday afternoon in March 1952 Roy and I 'plugged' school to see our team Hearts play Airdrie in a quarter-final replay of the Scottish Cup. As we waved to our pals and boarded the bus outside the school, we thought we'd worry about the headmaster tomorrow. What a game it was, standing behind the goal with a full house of over 40,000 fans. Willie Bauld scored a hat-trick and was simply brilliant as Hearts won 6-4. Waiting at the bus stop after the game, the familiar face of Jimmy Mackie popped out of the queue. We saw him, but did he see us? The next day at school everyone wanted to know about the game. Later on in the science room, Mr Newton called me up to his desk – I thought he was going to explain something regarding science. Quietly he asked, 'Enjoy the game Gibson?' To this day I am certain he knew Roy and I were there.

Another early match I recall was one winter's day when Winchburgh Albion played at Airth in the Scottish Juvenile Cup. The weather was awful, pouring with rain, and the game should never been played, but it was a big cup-tie and I seem to recall the whole town made the trip to Airth. As a kid, I managed to watch the game from inside the bus. While it wasn't easy to see the game over the heads of the supporters, it was cosy and dry. Most of the crowd were soaked to the skin and freezing to boot. Nobody should have been asked to play in all that mud. The Albion ran themselves to a standstill and were hanging on, but poor finishing and the appalling conditions prevented Airth from scoring on a number of occasions. I didn't realise it at the time but an old Airth committee man had announced there were still four minutes to go – I always thought it was the referee who had the watch. The Winchburgh crowd had been calling time for at least three minutes, tempers were rising and the referee was starting to get plenty of earache, particularly as some of the supporters had bet their week's wages on the outcome of the match.

The last four minutes took an eternity; could the Albion hold out for a draw and get a replay at Winchburgh? Into injury time and the crowd were baying for the ref's blood. As they were starting to climb over the wire rope around the touchline, the Albion linesman shouted at the ref to check his watch. Following another attack the Albion cleared the ball towards the halfway line and the ref blew his whistle. The Winchburgh crowd let out a roar thinking it was the final whistle, but it died in their throats when the ref ran over with his notebook and pen in his hand, took the linesman's name and dismissed him from the game! Isaac Turnbull, the Albion secretary, took over as linesman and the crowd was going crazy. Isaac was shouting for the committee men to spread out along the touchline to stop the supporters from encroaching onto the field. Eventually the ref started the game with a dropped ball, an Albion player got his foot to the ball and tried to belt it towards the half-way line. It cannoned off one of the Airth players and rebounded towards their right winger, who met it first time from a narrow angle. Unfortunately for the Albion he didn't connect properly and, instead of a hard rising shot, the ball bobbled along the ground past the unsuspecting goalkeeper. There was a stunned silence, broken only when the referee blew his whistle, first for the goal then for time. The Winchburgh crowd on the far side broke onto the pitch and the committee members were helpless as the mob made for the referee. Two or three idiots had wild kicks at him before one of the supporters stomped out of the mob, lifted him clear off his feet with a right hander to the jaw and knocked him out. Older supporters had tears in their eyes at what they were witnessing – it was a very sad day for Winchburgh and its football team, but one I have never forgotten.

It was time to gauge if the hours of practice with the tanner ba would yield a positive result. I went with my school pal Alex Petty to Armadale Thistle junior ground for an under-15 county schoolboys' trial match. Along with thirty other young hopefuls I was excited and nervous, but confident of doing well in my first trial. My confidence didn't last too long as I didn't make the starting line and together with about eight other kids I was on the bench. At half-time the schoolteacher made a few changes, but I stayed on the bench. With about ten minutes remaining the centre forward was injured and the teacher looked along the line. I was the only kid left. 'What's your name?' 'Gibson, sir.' 'Okay, on you go.' I was a 4-foot 6-inch left-winger at the time, around 6 stone and soaking wet. The opposition centre half was the Scottish schoolboy captain, to me he looked like a man and I never got a kick. However, with just two minutes to go we gained a corner. The ball came over, deflected off a defender and fell to me, about 10 yards out. Here was my chance of glory. Unfortunately it arrived at my right foot, the one I stand on. I took one almighty swipe to try and hit it as hard as I could. Just as you need the gods to shine on you the ball struck a divot, I missed it completely and fell on my arse. Feeling stupid and embarrassed I slowly got to my feet, looked towards the teacher and heard him scream – too loudly in my opinion – 'Who the hell sent that idiot for a trial?'

Of all the kids who played that day, and some were schoolboy internationals, I was the only boy to make it as a professional footballer. However, I started to suffer badly with an inferiority complex, partly because of my height, but mainly as a direct result of that teacher's attitude. Prior to that trial, I was enthusiastic and not a great worrier at all. I also went for a trial in Edinburgh, meeting the townies, and they were all talking to each other and oozing confidence. Here was I, a wee quiet kid of fifteen from the sticks well out of my comfort zone, hoping to let my feet do the talking. So to all dads and grandads, when you watch your kids play, don't be overly critical. You never know how your kid may turn out...

3

Hibernian Come Calling

As the years passed and my modest schooling was drawing to a close, at fifteen I had to find a job. 'A trade, my son, is what is required,' said my dad. 'Never mind this football fantasy. Only one or two in a hundred ever make it as a footballer.' It was an understandable comment for any father to make, so my pal Alex Pettie and I became labourers at the oil works. Wattie Reid from my paper round days was the gaffer. He gave Alex and I a large tin of battleship-grey paint to cover the railings alongside the railway line. After about two weeks Alex and I had more paint on us than the railings, but I was fortunate that an opportunity soon arose as a carpenter. So I started a five-year apprenticeship on a building site in Edinburgh. To be frank, I learnt little as a carpenter, but I learnt a lot more at lunch times. The five-a-sides were again part of my football education. I enjoyed the camaraderie with the older guys, the jokes and especially the 'educational' tips from my elders. 'Play the way you are facing son, one touch and move.' It had to be an Irishman who gave me one of the most important bits of guidance I ever received. With his bonnet turned back to front to prevent it blowing away, Peter Toner said, 'Davie, one of these days someone is going to give you a hard time. Wait until he gets close to tackle you, then kick the ball straight at his bollocks!' Who needs coaching when you get tips like that? I must admit that years later, it definitely worked. So thanks again to all the plumbers, electricians, labourers and bricklayers who made up the team every lunch break – every bit of advice I received I never forgot.

My passion for the game continued in December 1954 when I went with Alex Pettie to see Scotland play Hungary at Hampden Park. We managed to buy tickets but couldn't get transport, so we caught a Scottish supporters' bus near Winchburgh that came from Edinburgh. The match was nearly abandoned, as it had been frosty for a few days and they had to put straw on the pitch. Johnny Mackenzie, who was a flying right-winger, ran so fast once he ended up in the straw beside the pitch. I was hoping he might stay there injured so that my hero Willie Bauld, who was a reserve, might get on. Captain and right-back Willie Cunningham kicked lumps out of Mate Fenyvesi, their winger, to no avail and Scotland lost 4-2, with Tommy Ring and Bobby Johnstone scoring. What an experience to witness the Hungarians at first hand just a year after seeing them on television – the majestic Ferenc Puskás, Nándor Hidegkuti and Sándor Kocsis in front of 113,000 supporters.

The next stage of my development was playing for the Winchburgh Oil Works team. The sides mainly comprised players between the ages of sixteen and forty-five – fortunately I was the sixteen-year-old. You certainly didn't need a huge amount of talent to shine in this company. If you could run you were a star – the old boys couldn't catch you. Our captain was Paddy Clarke, a rough, tough, very aggressive eighteen-year-old. My good fortune held when a challenge match was thrown out against the Pumpherston works team. In the first game we scored six goals and I managed a hat-trick. A week or two later we played the return match at Pumpherston's magnificent junior ground, which looked like Wembley compared to what I was used to. The secretary of Livingston United, would you believe his name was also D. Gibson, was watching. We put another six past them and I scored another hat-trick. Mr Gibson liked what he saw and asked me to sign for 'Livvy', one of the elite secondary juvenile under-21 clubs in the county.

In Scottish Juvenile football, if you were knocked out in the first or second round of the Juvenile Cup, you were automatically entered into the Lady Darling Cup, which was a consolation tournament. I played in that latter Cup during my first (1954/55) season when we beat Port Glasgow Rangers in the final at Armadale Thistle. The following year new players arrived to replace the lads who had moved on to the junior ranks. What a team we turned out, including Davie Kidd, Peter Smith, Tommy Hill, the Murphy brothers, centre forward Walter McWilliams and Willie York, our super captain. We completed the entire season undefeated, winning 48 out of 49 games played, scoring 356 goals in the process and we swept the board, victorious in the League, the County Cup, the Fraser Cup and the McQueen Cup. Our success culminated in a 6-1 thrashing of Denny and Dunipace Rovers in the 1956 Scottish Juvenile Cup final at Edinburgh. Although Denny took the lead in the first half we came storming back, with two each from Warwick Black, McWilliams and York. I was pleased with my performance, reflected in one of the reports: 'His lack of inches does not prevent him from going into the tackle, while his perfect passes can spilt a defence wide open.'

As the team bus made its way out of the Old Meadowbank Stadium after the final, I asked one of the committee men if it could be routed through Winchburgh. On reaching the main street, then left past the old rows, I was disappointed there was not a soul in sight. Past the railway station, right at the bowling club, where was everybody? Along the front rows I had forgotten it was the local Gala Day. All the villagers were sitting around the football field, where I'd played Cowboys and Indians not so long ago. Streamers were draped across the road and, as we made our way along the front rows, everyone left their seats to get a closer look at the Cup. They clapped and cheered until we disappeared at the end of the village, a wonderful moment I'll never forget.

Thanks to my team-mates my career was starting to take shape and I'm grateful to them all for their help during that phase of my football journey. I've often wondered why I was the one to go on and make it in the pro ranks when I felt I was way down in the pecking order in terms of ability. There were four lads in particular that I felt talented enough to progress further.

Livingston United F.C., 1955/56, with our haul of trophies. Inset left: Dave Murphy, right: Barney Rice. Back row, left to right: Davie Kidd, Jimmy Murphy, John Proudfoot, Tommy Hill, Peter Smith, Warwick Black. Front row: Tam Hunter, myself, Walter McWilliams, Willie York, William Murray.

Aged seventeen in 1956, holding the Scottish Juvenile Cup won by Livingston.

Firstly, Walter 'Gunner' McWilliams was a goalscoring machine, notching over 100 goals that season. Walter signed for Hibernian but only played a couple of games before moving on to Cowdenbeath. In goal, secondly, was John Proudfoot, who also joined Hibs but didn't quite make it against fierce competition from Jackie Wren and Lawrie Leslie. We were 1-0 up in the McQueen Cup final against Westrigg Bluebell when a penalty was awarded against us. As their captain came up to take it, John took a step to his right, leaving an enormous gap to his left. The captain took the bait and hit his shot to John's left. John took off to produce a wonder save and we went on to win the Cup that night. Years later I mentioned John's positional plan to both Gordon Banks and Peter Shilton, but I'm not sure if either used his unusual ploy.

During that final I suffered the worst injury of my career. I slid in to try and tackle their big, strong left half, who promptly fell on top of me. The trainer came on and gave my knee a rub and after the game it felt okay. However, the next morning I got out of bed and fell over – the ligament in my knee had gone. I had treatment from a physio at Broxburn and was out for about six weeks. I never broke a bone throughout my entire time as a professional, but then I didn't go in for many tackles!

Thirdly, Peter Smith, a constructive and destructive right half, if there is such a footballing label, scored over forty goals. I didn't score many goals from midfield at that time and remember we were 11-0 up in one game when we were awarded a penalty. I was given it to score but Peter, as regular taker, went off in a right huff! Last but not least, Davie Kidd was a magnificent full back with nine Scottish Youth caps to his name.

There was an abundance of scouts at the Juvenile Cup final and Peter and Davie promptly signed for Hearts. Their wage was £5-6 a week part-time, training on Tuesdays and Thursdays. Tommy Walker, their manager, also came to see me twice and made an offer of £7 but only if I played in the first team – otherwise it was £4 a week. I couldn't work out why he was offering me less, but it was the first time I learnt that clubs offered the least money they thought they could get away with. It was also Hearts' policy to farm youngsters out to the juniors to make them bigger and stronger. Smith and Kidd went to Dalkeith Juniors, and then trained with the reserves in the evening. Around that time I went to the pictures with Walter McWilliams, who by then had signed for Hibernian. He told me that their manager Hugh Shaw had been asking about me. At first I was in two minds about signing professional, as I was hoping I might win a Scottish Youth cap, having already been a reserve. In the event Hibs offered me £9 a week and I could train and play with the reserves straight away, so there was no junior football, which also appealed to me. Before I made my mind up I saw my uncle in the village. I told him about the two offers and he said, 'Christ and you're thinking about it!' I actually didn't sign for Hibs because of the money – it was purely because Walter was already there, so he shaped my destiny. I signed as a professional in July 1956, a few weeks after the Juvenile Cup final.

Around this time I met up regularly with half a dozen potential footballers from the big smoke, Edinburgh. We all socialised after a game on Saturday nights at the Edinburgh Palais. Typically, we'd spend the evening discussing football for about two and a half hours, hoping that one of the lassies would come over to talk to you. I

First photograph on signing professional
for Hibernian in 1956.

wasn't used to all these townies in the early days, coming from the miners' rows. One evening, when it looked as though a gaggle of girls would descend on me, I pretended I was with the girl standing next to me. Her name was Jeanette and she went on to marry Lawrie Leslie, so she played her cards right in the end.

As a group we also enjoyed some great five-a-sides on Gullane beach every Sunday during the summer. It included Billy Hunter and Jimmy Robertson, who played for Motherwell with Bobby Roberts, who later joined me at Leicester City, Alan Anderson and Andy Bowman of Hearts, and Alan Robertson and Jimmy Kane of Hibs. Throw in Andy Cunningham, Johnny Rowley and Felix Traynor of that era. What an education it was and not a coach in sight. Most of the lads made it to the pro ranks so we must have been doing something right.

Sammy Kean, an old professional with the club from the 1940s, was in charge of pre-season training at Hibernian. Together with twenty other youngsters, we walked and jogged our way from Easter Road to Portobello, a seaside resort about 5 miles away. When we arrived at the beach I wondered how Sammy realised the tide was out, as he marked out 50 yards square in the sand. Then the really hard work began. Young Pat Hughes was first off and every 10 yards another followed. You ran one side of the square then jogged the other. After about five laps and tiring rapidly, my foot became tangled in my heavy tracksuit and I took a 'header' into the sand. Exhausted and embarrassed, Sammy came over to see if I was okay, but I thought my career

I'm the odd one out on holiday with Motherwell lads Bobby Roberts, Billy Hunter and Jimmy Robertson at the Tartan Bar, Jersey, 1960.

Scoring for Hibs V. Bo'ness United in a friendly, 1956. Who said I was hopeless in the air?

was over before it had started. Thankfully the five-a-side soon began and that was my environment, thanks to all those years with the wee tanner ba. Fortunately Sammy took a shine to me – he was always cheerful and gave me plenty of encouragement.

One of my first appearances at Easter Road was a public trial match between Hibernian 'A' and 'B' sides. Captaining the 'A' side in his fifteenth season for the club was the legendary Gordon Smith. While everything had happened so quickly, I managed to settle into the game and we achieved an honourable 1-1 draw. The local press reported, 'Baby-faced David Gibson, at 17 the youngest player on the field, could be another Bobby Johnstone. Of the same cheekie chappie mould, Gibson has a shrewd football brain and confidence galore.'

It was hugely flattering to be compared with Bobby Johnstone, but I was just a kid and didn't feel overly confident. I knew there was a lot of hard work to put in, especially as there was some criticism at the time that I couldn't last a game and lacked stamina. One of the old boys I worked with as a carpenter was Jimmy McLean, who played for Hibs years before me and went on to captain Stirling Albion after the war. He suggested I do a wee bit of training at Winchburgh in addition to the Tuesday and Thursday evenings with Hibs. So I did press-ups in the miners' rows for about quarter of an hour, and then under lamplight sprinted from the goalmouth to the eighteen-yard box of the football pitch with a young lad called 'Chippy' Gibb. Chippy was only about ten or eleven, and I would give him a start to the six-yard box and try and beat him – it was good company for me. That definitely helped me before I joined the Army and became even stronger.

The forward line of the late 1940s and 1950s comprised the 'Famous Five', Gordon Smith, Bobby Johnstone, Lawrie Reilly, Eddie Turnbull and Willie Ormond, all capped many times for Scotland. The names trip off the tongue for every Hibee, as it was undoubtedly the most famous forward line in the club's history. The abundantly talented five ensured Hibs were one of the most successful sides in Scotland, both sporting wise and at the turnstiles. The League title was captured three times (1948, 1951 and 1952) and it could have been four, but for Rangers edging ahead on the goal average system in 1953.

In March 1955 Bobby Johnstone was transferred to Manchester City and on 15 August 1956 I made my first-team debut in the League Cup at home to Falkirk. The forward line then read Smith, Gibson, Reilly, Turnbull, Ormond. Not the 'Famous Five' any longer – more like the 'Famous Four and a Half!' I had to pinch myself; I was in the company of players I had shouted at a couple of years ago when they played against my team Hearts. However, it was no fairy tale; in all honesty I was overawed, I ran about a lot but never got a kick, we lost 1-0 and after two games I was back in the stiffs learning my craft.

Hibernian: Wren, Brown, McClelland, Higgins, Grant, Laing, Smith, Gibson, Reilly, Turnbull, Ormond.

I did make an impact in the reserves with a young pal of mine, Scottish schoolboy international Tommy Kilbride – we made up the left-wing partnership. Another friendly trial match was arranged behind closed doors in which the reserves beat the seniors 3-1. Tommy and I were on the same wavelength and a local reporter wrote,

Man of the match was that bundle of tricks, young Davie Gibson. His every move had the hallmark of class. A few extra pounds on that spare frame and young Davie will be a world-beater. A Gibson goal would have been a fitting climax to a top class display. Highlight of the night was the Gibson-Kilbride movement which pegged back the Seniors' lead, scored after twenty minutes by Baker off a perfect Preston through pass. Gibson and Kilbride zig-zagged their way up the left wing in a manner which could not have been bettered by the all-conquering Brazilians. Gibson squared the ball to Ken Allison, who smashed home a left-foot drive in twenty-eight minutes.

I continued my apprenticeship, still small but maturing, and gained more experience in the reserves with old pros like Tommy Preston and Bobby Combe. Tommy was a few years older than me and whenever Lawrie Reilly was injured would deputise at centre forward, but he could also play in my position, inside left. I used to gaze at Tommy, about 6 feet tall and heavily tanned. He looked magnificent and I thought I'd never get a game with Tommy on the books. He was a versatile player, elegant for a big guy, with a good touch and a loyal pro for Hibs.

Bobby Combe was another full international from the Famous Five era – he could play left half or inside left, was another versatile pro and a lovely wee fella. A couple of years after Sammy Kean retired, Bobby took over the reserves and helped me a lot in my development. I remember a game against Celtic at Parkhead when it was common practice for the inside forward to mark the wing half. I was up against Ian White, who later played at Leicester, then Southampton. Bobby was playing against a young kid called Paddy Crerand. I never got a kick of the ball – White stuck to me like shit to a blanket. After about half an hour Bobby suggested we swap places but it didn't get any easier against Paddy, even though Bobby had tried to help me.

Bobby was taking all the part-timers for training one night at Easter Road, about eighteen of us. Harry Swan, who had been the chairman since the 1930s, and the directors must have been meeting at the club. They were standing in the tunnel on the half-way line while we were away by the far corner flag. Bobby was keen to show them we were happy in our work, so quick as a flash Walter McWilliams started singing the Al Jolson lyrics, 'I'm just wild about Harry, Harry's wild about me.' Bobby's chest was pumping with pride. Then Walter, who had a very sharp wit, came up with another: 'Swanee, how I love you...' Of course Harry loved it and was most impressed with Bobby's young charges.

During this time I was struggling to break into the first team and my brittle confidence had all but eroded, so I asked Bobby for his advice. He knew a reporter who worked in the *Edinburgh Dispatch* and arranged for him to write an article, 'What happened to Davie Gibson?' I wasn't a regular for a long time but Bobby always encouraged me.

Hugh Higgins was a wily, tough wing half who played behind me in the reserves and looked after me on the pitch. He was a ginger-haired dynamo and a real bustler. He was a terrific lad for me – if anyone kicked me, Hugh was there. After he'd run around for about a quarter of an hour you couldn't miss him, as he started to sweat and became redder and redder. We were both part-timers – Hugh came from Falkirk on the bus for training and I joined him at Winchburgh, so I got to know him well. When I was injured I watched him in the reserves once at Aberdeen. You could never fault Hugh for effort but our trainer Jimmy McColl, who didn't seem to like the lad, moaned about him. Fred Martin was watching, an ex-Aberdeen and Scotland goalkeeper from the 1950s, and I heard him say, 'Who's that ginger-haired guy, what a player!' Hugh probably fell out with the hierarchy as he could speak up for himself and moved to Third Lanark in 1958. He then had a short spell with Dunfermline, but sadly suffered a bad ligament injury and was never same player again.

Lawrie Leslie was another working his way through the ranks and we were just kids when we toured Spain with the club in the late 1950s. We played Barcelona one night and got beaten by four or five. Jimmy McColl had a go at Lawrie after the game. We were sharing a room and Lawrie's wife Jeanette had just had a baby boy. He said to me, 'Davie, I wish I was back home.' He was a nice guy and I tried to tell him not to let it bother him – after all they were a decent Spanish team. Like most trainers or managers, Jimmy, who was a fine centre forward with Hibs in the 1920s, moaned whenever we lost and always took it out on someone.

Lawrie was a big, strapping bugger and a brave keeper who went on to play five times for Scotland. Jeanette said he put courage before wisdom, like so many keepers of that era. He moved to Airdrie in 1959 and the biggest heartbreak of his career was when he dived at the feet of an Ayr forward the week before he was due to play against England at Wembley in 1961. Lawrie was carried off and taken to hospital, where eleven stitches were inserted into a serious eyebrow gash. Manager Ian McColl withdrew him from the Scotland side even though the doctor said he was fit to play. It was a huge disappointment to Lawrie, as he was desperate to play. In the event Frank Haffey deputised and of course infamously conceded nine against the best England team I ever saw.

Hibernian typically occupied mid-table in the league during the late 1950s, but reached the Scottish Cup final in April 1958, albeit losing by the odd goal to Clyde. It wasn't until the 1958/59 season that I was given an extended run in the first team and played in twenty-five games. One of the most memorable was in December 1958, when we beat Partick Thistle 4-0 at home. Joe Baker and I both scored twice, my first goals in senior football. The *Sunday Mail* reported,

> For once Joe Baker doesn't steal all the limelight because a new star looks like arising. The first goal was a nice piece of workmanship, the second a little work of art. From just outside the penalty area and with the Thistle defenders wondering what he had in mind, Gibson let fly with a left-foot shot that spelt goal every inch of its glorious way. A laddie who can tame a ball in a flash, wiggle a hip like a Bardot and spray around the passes that others love, this boy David is here to stay.

Unsurprisingly, that was the only time I was ever mentioned in the same breath as Brigitte Bardot!

We also beat Thistle in the third round of the Scottish Cup, again at Easter Road in February 1959. Joe was out for a few weeks with a bad ankle injury and Des Fox,

Scoring in the snow against Raith Rovers in January 1959. 'Hibs second goal was the climax to a brilliant solo run by inside right Davie Gibson.'

a young inside forward, came in. Des was a playmaker and led the line well at centre forward in a 4-1 victory. A newspaper reported the game thus:

> The most illuminating feature of Hibs victory was the team can play high grade football even without Joe Baker, their 18 year-old centre forward. I am thinking particularly of Fox and Davie Gibson. The fresh complexioned Gibson is an inside forward of ability. His positional sense and distribution, his constant endeavour to play as part of a fast moving line, stamp him as unselfish and a player with a future. There were all sorts of attacking permutations; Fox-Aitken-Gibson, Ormond-Fox-Gibson, Smith-Aitken-Gibson, Ormond-Smith-Gibson etc., but they all had one name in common – Gibson.

We were through to the quarter-finals of the Cup and played Third Lanark in March 1959. Joe Baker was back in the side but you could tell he wasn't 100 per cent fit. You can't blame Hugh Shaw for playing him, he was that good a goalscorer, but we lost 2-1. I missed a sitter when I dived in for a header and knocked it over the bar. On the bus after the game Eddie Turnbull, the captain, said to Joe, 'Son, don't you ever play football again when you're not fit.' Like any young guy, Joe was desperate to play, but Eddie, the senior pro, was not impressed.

I was picked the same month (16 March) to play in a friendly at Ibrox for a Scotland XI against the Scottish League. It was my first representative honour, a great thrill, and I was selected when John Hewie was injured. John was normally a full-back, but his

Hibernian V. Third Lanark. I miss a sitter and my face says it all.

club Charlton had at the time been experimenting him at inside forward. John White, of whom more later, was the star of the League side, scoring a hat-trick on a misty evening. In fact John scored twice inside the opening twenty minutes, as we struggled to find any rhythm. John Colrain reduced the deficit for us on twenty-one minutes, then Dave Mackay, with a powerful first-time strike, and Graham Leggat eased us in front before half-time. When Colrain scored his second shortly after the interval the League appeared a beaten team, but rallied with a hat-trick from Andy Kerr then John White with his third. Remarkably John Colrain also completed his hat-trick but by then it was too late. The 6-5 score-line was no doubt considered a thrilling game by the 40,000 spectators, but was a huge disappointment to me.

I was too young, too nervous and the game completely passed me by. I remember sitting in the tub afterwards feeling sorry for myself and it must have showed. The chap sitting next to me turned and said, 'Don't be too disappointed son, your time will come.' In all my years as a pro I never forgot that or who said it – Graham Leggat. As I was about to leave the dressing room, the Scottish trainer, I think it was Dawson Walker, posed me a football question. 'Davie, who was the last Scottish player to get two caps on the same day?' 'Don't know,' I replied innocently. 'You are son, your first and your bloody last.' I think he was kidding! There was half an hour's coverage of the match on television and when I arrived home my mother, who had eagerly been watching, asked if I played, as everyone had been mentioned but me. Perhaps if I had been commented on, it might not have been too complimentary, as I was hopeless. At the time I wasn't sure if I wanted to carry on – my deep insecurity remained and a year later that friendly match came back to haunt me.

Scotland: Brown, Parker, Caldow, Cumming, Evans, Mackay, Scott, Collins, Colrain, Gibson, Leggat.

Scottish League: Wallace, McKay, Baird, Smith, McCallum, McCann, McEwan, White, Kerr, Gray, Ormond.

4

National Service Intervenes

National Service was formalised in 1949 as a peacetime form of conscription. Men were exempt if they worked in essential services – unfortunately, football was not one of them. Consequently in July 1960 I received my call-up papers and reported to the Medical Centre at Edinburgh. Two years in the Army was not my idea of fulfilling my dream as a pro, especially as I was still striving to break through into the Hibs first team. I was called forward for my medical examination, and a stroke of fortune came my way, as one of the panel recognised me as a young footballer. After breezing through the formalities the medical staff member, on reaching the final examination, studied the form and asked me, 'Have you ever had a serious health problem?' 'No.' 'Are you sure, think again?' The penny dropped, he was giving me the opportunity to find an excuse to fail the medical. I replied, 'When I was young I had problems with my ears.' 'Fine, for hearing problems you need to see a specialist for further examinations.' Two weeks later a date was arranged for me to see the specialist. The lady gave me earphones and proceeded to turn some dials that emitted various sounds. 'Nod when you hear any sound.' I heard them all but as I was offered the chance to escape my service, I nodded a few times and kept silent at other times. A week later a letter arrived – 'PASS!'

I had met a sergeant at the Medical Centre, but didn't realise at the time he was a recruiting sergeant for the King's Own Scottish Borderers regiment and knew my background. He explained he could arrange for me to be stationed at Berwick so that I could travel home every weekend to play for Hibs. There was nothing wrong with my hearing when he told me that – 23805586 Private David Wedderburn Gibson, First Battalion, K.O.S.B. here I come. In late July, together with twenty other recruits, we duly arrived at Berwick for training and were kitted out then placed in our living quarters. It was four to a room and my fellow 'inmates' were Robert Wilson, Neil Duncan and Jock Sangster.

At around 5.30 a.m. on my first morning a corporal entered the room and, after banging his baton on the radiator next to our beds, hollered, 'Okay, you shower of shit. Hands off cocks and on with socks.' Feet on the floor, the four of us slowly manoeuvred ourselves out of bed and when he disappeared put our legs back under the blanket. Twenty seconds later, he marched in again bellowing, 'Do you think I came up the

Clyde in a banana boat, get your arses out of bed.' My immediate thought was, mum, what have I let myself in for, will I ever survive two years?

After just six weeks of training Robert bought himself out, which was feasible if you were a regular. Neil was a local lad who made it as the adjutant's batsman and is still a good friend. Jock, the tallest man in the squad, became Sergeant Major in the battalion, served twenty-two years and was a natural soldier. Whenever I tried to bull my boots, it was so much effort I fell asleep but help was at hand. When I arrived back to my billet at night I often found my boots bulled, shining in front of me – you could see your face in them. Attached was a note; 'Gibson, this is how your boots should be bulled.' Jock had looked after me.

I had four weeks of basic training at Berwick but never took to Army life. Fortunately, football was never far away. While playing for the unit team at Berwick, the First Battalion team stationed in Berlin came over and toured the local Borders, playing various matches, including our unit team. We gave them a run for their money in a side that included Tommy White, brother of John, Tommy Mackle, a very clever left-winger with a thunderbolt of a shot who went on to play for Celtic, and little Pat Foley, a tricky right-winger who played for Alloa.

I was soon shipped out to Berlin to play for the Battalion football team on my basic pay of £1 a week. I boarded the night train with a sergeant and private on the first part of our journey to London. Two other Scots were in our compartment, on their way to London looking for work. The conversation soon turned to football, with one of them rattling on about how good the international team was. 'I'm sorry,' I replied, 'I don't think Scotland will ever have a good team.' I explained how a young lad I knew played in a Scotland team against a Scottish League XI at Ibrox the previous year. Granted he didn't play too well that night, but there was no encouragement for him whatsoever. 'He picked up his boots and walked out of the stadium. If you treat youngsters like that, they have no chance.' 'Wait a minute,' said the Glaswegian, 'I was at that game, what was the young lad's name?' 'Oh a young man who played for Hibs called Davie Gibson.' I've never forgotten his exact words in reply, precise and to the point; 'I remember him, he'll never be a footballer as long as there's a hole in his arse!' Between him and that schoolteacher a few years prior, did they know something I didn't?

In all honesty Army life helped me enormously in my football career. Playing for the Battalion team in Berlin, the lads looked to me for help and guidance and that in turn gave me confidence. We were a pretty useful outfit, reaching the semi-final of the B.A.O.R Cup before we lost to a Leicestershire regiment. One day, we smuggled our way into the Berlin Stadium and had our picture taken on the same track where Jesse Owens, that magnificent American sprinter, won his gold medal in the 1936 Olympics. After a few months the battalion was transferred to Edinburgh. Great news for me – I could play for Hibs again. I was based in the Officers' Mess as a waiter and put on about five pounds in weight, although the two were not necessarily connected.

Peter Rooke was the Army adjutant and took a shine to me, as he ran the football team. He was a lovely man but no pushover. When the battalion was leaving Edinburgh on one occasion, Peter had us all cleaning the barracks for four weeks, every nook and cranny. I remember asking him why the hell we needed to be so thorough. His reply

Playing in Berlin for K.O.S.B. against Dragoon Guards in the Army Cup, November 1960 (number 8). The Olympic Stadium is in the background.

The King's Own Scottish Borderers side at Berlin in 1960. Back row: Peters, Storey, Moffat, Broadledey, English, Gordon. Front row: Foley, myself, Sneddon, Ford, Mackle.

Consigned to a stint at Aden during my National Service in 1962, I find time to practice with the local youngsters. Note their bare feet and the oilfield in the background.

has stayed with me to this day – 'Gibson, leave it as you expect to find it.' I've tried to pass that philosophy on to my children and grandchildren and it's come in very handy over the years.

The directors at Easter Road thought they could ply Peter with whisky and soften him up, so that any time they rang up he would agree to release me. Peter was more educated than that and when one day they asked for me to be released to play for the reserves, Peter politely told them he was keeping me to play in his first team.

Unfortunately, after a few months we were posted to Aden – where the hell was Aden? Once more my career was on hold. The battalion actually departed without yours truly, thanks to a few mysterious ailments I manufactured. I managed to stay in 'Blighty' for another few weeks before the authorities caught up with me and I was on my way. I soon discovered Aden was a legacy of our dwindling empire, situated at the tip of Saudi Arabia, notable for sand, lack of shade and the dreaded flies. The companies were on call at 4.30 a.m. before it became too hot and, having already been there for six weeks, everyone else in my battalion looked as brown as a berry except me. On my first parade, out walked Regimental Sergeant Major 'Dusty' Murdoch. You could hear him a mile away as he bellowed prior to inspection, 'Will the milk bottle step forward!' I stood there extremely embarrassed and must have resembled a snowman among those tanned bodies. Even when swimming I wore a hat, jeans and a t-shirt, but still managed to get myself badly burnt.

Some years ago when we were living in Leicester, my wife Mavis noticed a small mark on the side of my face. It turned out to be skin cancer, 'basal cell carcinoma', and I'm sure my time in Aden was a contributory factor. I went into hospital and had it successfully removed. A couple of years later another appeared, so I had the same procedure. As I was lying on the operating table the young lady surgeon told me that, as a young girl, she and three of her friends used to stand by the tunnel at Filbert Street where the teams came out. 'Mr Gibson, you were my hero.' I replied that someone told me once to admire their heroes from afar, as when you meet them close up they usually let you down. 'Never in your case Mr Gibson!' When I arrived home and told Mavis this lovely story, she thought I'd made it up. I still need regular check-ups and if the specialists find anything similar they freeze it with liquid nitrogen. If only we had used sun cream.

5

European Adventure

In 1955 Hibernian was the first club side to play in European competition when invited to participate in the European Cup. The English Football League persuaded champions Chelsea not to enter, claiming it to be an insignificant competition! Hibs were happy to oblige, as Easter Road was one of the first Scottish grounds to be blessed with floodlights. Four years later an invitation was extended to compete in the Inter-Cities Fairs Cup, established to promote trade fairs between European cities. Edinburgh hosted an international fair at the time so it provided another opportunity to test us against Continental opposition. In October 1960 we drew Lausanne in the first round. Lausanne promptly withdrew, as a number of their players would have been away on international duty. We then faced Barcelona, arguably the best team in Europe, in the next round and managed a hugely creditable 4–4 draw at the Camp Nou. We then defeated them 3–2 amid chaotic scenes at Easter Road in the return tie against all the odds, although unfortunately I didn't play in either leg. In April 1961 we were up against crack Italian outfit Roma in the semi, drawing 2-2 at home in a bad-tempered affair.

I was released by the Army for the return fixture a week later after a decent performance against Clyde, which we won 4-0. With 22,000 fanatical Italian supporters baying for our blood, the tie was accompanied by a tremendous thunderstorm – quite a baptism in European football for me. It was also obvious to me early on that they were a very talented outfit, although only a superb save by Cudicini prevented us taking the lead from a Sammy Baird effort. However, after twenty minutes Argentinian striker Pedro Manfredini put them in front, having missed a sitter a few minutes earlier. We weren't playing badly at the time and when Bobby Kinloch blasted the ball into the net twelve minutes later, it was a well-merited equaliser. Our good form carried into the second half, when Joe Baker picked the ball up midway inside the Roma half. He set off on a mazy run past three defenders before rifling a low shot past Cudicini to stun the home crowd into silence. Just two minutes later, Bobby Kinloch's measured cross was met firmly by Joe's forehead. We were 3-1 up, not exactly cruising but in dreamland – could it last? Sadly, we tired in the second half, defended too deep and Manfredini pulled one back with a penalty, then Lojacono grabbed an equaliser. In truth, were it not

Hibernian squad at Turnhouse Airport in 1960 en route to close-season tour of Europe. Players, left to right: John MacLeod, Willie Muirhead, myself, Bobby Johnstone, John Young, Duncan Faulkner, Jim Scott, Bobby Kinloch, Jackie Plenderleith, Jock Buchanan, Willie Ormond, John Fraser, Joe McClelland, John Baxter and Eddie Turnbull. Manager Hugh Shaw is holding the newspaper, far right.

for some great goalkeeping by Ronnie Simpson and another glaring miss by Manfredini, the Italians would have been through but the tie ended 3-3.

Hibernian: Simpson, Fraser, Davin, Kinloch, Easton, Baird, MacLeod, Baker, Baxter, Gibson, Ormond.

Roma: Cudicini, Fontana, Corsini, Guiliano, Losi, Carpanesi, Orlando, Lojacono, Manfredini, Angelillo, Menichelli.

As away goals didn't count in those days, a coin would ordinarily have been tossed to decide the venue for the deciding play-off. However the directors actually agreed to return to Rome towards the end of May 1961 after having been given a financial guarantee. That was not a big surprise to us as Johnny MacLeod, myself and Ronnie Simpson threw a coin into the Trevi fountain on our visit, which of course meant you would return one day. However, it didn't mean you would get stuffed 6-0 as we did! It was our heaviest defeat in European competition, mainly due to the brilliance of Manfredini, who scored four of the six goals. It also came four weeks after our last game of the season and, with 50,000 passionate home supporters, the odds were always stacked against us.

From the play-off match I remember Juan Schiaffino, an inside forward who starred in the Uruguay team that won the World Cup in 1950. He was still a class act, albeit

Relaxing in the Mediterranean after the Roma Cup game; John MacLeod, Joe Davin, John Baxter, John Fraser, Jim Easton, Tommy Preston and myself.

coming to the end of his career. Another was midfielder Francisco Lojacono, who represented Argentina and Italy at international level. It was a terrific experience for me to play in Rome's Olympic stadium so early in my career. Roma went on to defeat Birmingham City in the final, which was held at the start of the following season.

Joe Baker was the star of our side, a fantastic player and special goalscorer. They say footballers are quicker today. Try telling that to anyone who watched Joe, the fastest player I ever played with. He rarely made a goal as he was always on the end of a move, belting it into the net. If you went for a one-two you'd never get it back. In 1959 he became the first footballer to be capped for England while playing for a club outside the English Football League. I'm sure the Italians spotted him when he played in the Roma ties, as the play-off was his last game for us before he signed for Torino with Denis Law. By 1962 Joe had moved to Arsenal and I played against him in August 1963 for Leicester at Filbert Street. We were 2-1 up after twenty-two minutes when Jack McClelland broke his collarbone in a collision with Ken Keyworth. Joe took over in goal – their top goalscorer – how did he get away with that? Even the players couldn't believe it, but I didn't mind as I helped myself to a couple of goals and we eventually beat them 7-2.

We had plenty of other decent players in the Hibernian team. Centre half Jim

My old pal Joe Baker (right) is beaten in goal by a shot from me in the 7-2 home rout against Arsenal in August 1963. Jimmy Magill and Ian Ure look distinctly unhappy.

Easton was an old-fashioned defender, hard but not dirty. Left back Joe McClelland was another tough 'thou shalt not pass' defender before the advent of overlapping full-backs. He wasn't great with the ball at his feet – it equally finished up in the stand – but he could tackle and win the ball cleanly. That was his job and he did it pretty well.

Mention of Joe's name reminds me of an unorthodox training session at Easter Road one evening. One of our trainers came up with the novel idea of a baseball game to make it a bit light-hearted. He handed out the bat, gloves etc., the corner flag was the base and we faced the pitch, where he marked out the other bases. He told us to run if we hit the ball, but if we missed after three strikes we were to run anyway. He stressed to all of us, 'When you hit the ball or if it's the third strike and you have to run, drop the bat. Don't run away with it in your hand and whatever you do, do not throw it backwards.' Joe McClelland was first batter and a wee fella called Jimmy Thomson was the catcher behind the base. Joe proceeded to miss the ball three times so started to run but forgot to drop the bat. As soon as he realised, instead of dropping it he threw the bat and it flew back like a boomerang. It hit Jimmy right in the face between the eyes, breaking his nose and completely knocking him out. End of the baseball experiment!

John Baxter was a tough left half in my time, not in the same league as Jim Baxter, but a very good, versatile pro. A loyal servant, he played over 300 times for the club. John Fraser came through with me and had the unenviable task of replacing Gordon Smith. He was quite tall, a solid right-winger who could fly a bit. He was also a good servant to Hibs, playing 275 games, and ended up playing at right-back.

Sammy Baird spent most of his career with Glasgow Rangers, either as an inside left or left half. He was signed in 1960 to replace Bobby Johnstone when he left the second time round and was with us for a couple of years. Sammy was another six-footer with a great touch, was comfortable on the ball, but could also dish it out. He was close to being dirty, but let's say he was hard.

Johnny MacLeod had pace to burn, like Joe Baker, and played four times for Scotland. He was energetic, comfortable on either wing and more a flyer than dribbler, although he wasn't afraid to take full-backs on. He was another under 5 feet 8 inches, where have these wee wingers gone in the modern game? Eric Stevenson was another I met during my early days and was more of a dribbling winger. He was also at ease on either wing, with two good feet. His first thought was always where is the full-back to take him on? Eric was elusive and could go past defenders inside or outside. A good pro with Hibs for a number of years, he scored 79 goals, a very tidy sum for a wide player.

That 1960/61 season I played just five first team matches, including the two Roma ties. There were plenty other youngsters playing three or four games in different positions, gradually developing in the first team. Then, on reaching maturity, we found the position we were best at. I was fighting with Kenny Allison, Des Fox, Jimmy Kane, Andy Aitken and Jimmy Harrower for one of the inside forward positions.

Being just midway through my National Service didn't help, but I was hopeful of an upturn in my fortunes when in August 1961 I was chosen to play for an Edinburgh Select XI to herald the start of the new season. Our opponents at Easter Road were the great Burnley side that almost won the double, losing to Tottenham in the FA Cup final. It was one of my most cherished memories for several reasons that I will explain later.

We again competed in the Fairs Cup during 1961/62 and, after overcoming the Portuguese side Belenenses 6-4 on aggregate, were drawn against Red Star Belgrade, the strongest club side in Yugoslavia. We experienced a pretty tortuous journey, caused by dense fog, taking thirty hours instead of ten. We started the final leg to reach Belgrade at 4.30 a.m. on the day of the game, far from ideal preparation, and it was no great surprise that we were no match for them in a 4-0 defeat. Add to the mix the German referee, who allowed the Red Star team to kick us off the park. He had plenty of opportunity to calm things down before Jim Easton brought down Sekularac in the second half. Sekularac leapt to his feet and started kicking and punching Jim, which the ref chose to ignore and sent Jim off! Just before the return leg in November 1961, Hugh Shaw resigned on the back of a string of dismal results in the League. In the event we made a decent fist of it at Easter Road but went down by a solitary goal.

First leg: Simpson, Fraser, McClelland, Grant, Easton, Davin, Stevenson, Cuthbert, Preston, Gibson, MacLeod.

Second leg: Muirhead, Fraser, McClelland, Davin, Easton, Hughes, Stevenson, Gibson, Baxter, Preston, MacLeod.

My abiding memory of those ties was attacking midfielder Dragoslav Sekularac. As the two teams were waiting in the corridor before the first leg, this swarthy, gipsy-looking guy stood adrift from everyone else. We all wondered who he was – it didn't take too long to find out. Early on, the floodlights went dim and the game had to be halted. A few balls were thrown onto the pitch for us to keep warm. Sekularac was flicking the ball over his head and volleying it into the goal – he had immaculate technical ability. Quick and crafty with creative skills, Sekularac was supremely confident throughout the match. In the years to come he became the biggest showman and crowd-pleaser in his country and one of the most significant footballers in the history of Red Star Belgrade. Unfortunately, he is also remembered for an infamous incident when, in 1962, he assaulted the referee in a League match and ended up serving an eighteen-month suspension. I knew there was something amiss with that guy in the tunnel and his reaction to Jim's tackle did him no favours.

Red Star were eventually eliminated in the semi-final by Barcelona. I always felt it a privilege to play against some of the greatest players in the world. Roma's Pedro Manfredini, who was Serie A top scorer in 1962/63, and Dragoslav Sekularac were definitely in that category, footballing legends, alongside the best I ever saw or played against.

Other than the two European ties, I only played once for the first team during the months of October and November 1961 and it seemed obvious to me that I wasn't in the club's plans. I'd been playing four or five times a week, so felt fit and strong. After a League Cup game at Easter Road, I was driven 50 miles to Duns to play two hours later for the Kosbies, so my stamina was no longer an issue. At twenty-three I was happy with my form and wanted to get settled with a club before being demobbed. I played in a challenge match at Tynecastle when the British Army defeated Hearts 3-0, reported as follows; 'Let's be perfectly frank and say Davie Gibson WAS the British Army. His role of general was executed so perfectly, so rewarding (one goal and one assist) that Monty's Irish eyes would have smiled and smiled at the sight.'

The following morning after breakfast I sat down with my Army team-mates and wrote requesting either a free transfer or to be put on the 'open to transfer' list. I don't think it came as a great shock to the club – Frank Osborne, the Fulham manager, had previously put in an unsuccessful bid for me along with Alex Young, who was at Hearts at the time. I knew Don Revie at Leeds had also been sniffing around. Hibs actually didn't need the cash, having sold Joe Baker and Johnny MacLeod for a combined fee of £100,000 during the close season, and needless to say my request was turned down.

6

Opportunity Knocks South of the Border

After that unhappy episode I did become a regular fixture in the first team and withdrew my transfer request, making twenty starts during the first half of the 1961/62 season. As it happened, fate intervened when we played Celtic at Parkhead ten days before Christmas 1961. Leicester City coach Bert Johnson, manager Matt Gillies and the directors were in Scotland scouting Pat Quinn, a super inside forward with Motherwell. Leicester had signed Mike Stringfellow earlier in the month from Third Division Mansfield. By half-time they didn't think Pat and Mike were suited to play together, so Bert nipped off to see the match at Parkhead and definitely thought I was suitable. We were a bit unfortunate to lose 4-3 in a close-fought match, which Rex Kingsley of the *Sunday Mail* reported on:

> Hibs' chief attacking menace was Davie Gibson, the laddie with the tram ticket legs. Maybe he looks like a corner flag somebody's shoved a jersey over, but that corner flag carries two talking feet, a nimble brain and a flag that's always a danger. Once again he showed what a ball player can do with a defence.

Bert had fortuitously stumbled across me and told Matt to forget the deal with Pat, he had seen the ideal partner for Mike. Shortly afterwards I played for the Army at Redford Barracks against the Royal Signals, and Matt Gillies and Leicester chairman Len Shipman came to have a look at me for themselves. After the game I was driven by car to Winchburgh with both Matt and Hibs' new manager Walter Galbraith so that I could discuss the move with my parents. During negotiations I asked Matt if he felt I was fast enough for the First Division. His reply encouraged me: 'You're quick over the first few yards, that's all that really matters.' My father suggested I delay signing for a day or two – 'Have a look around Leicester first. Remember your whole career is at stake,' he said.

Arriving at Leicester station on the Friday afternoon, I was driven to the Belmont Hotel. That evening I met up with Mr Needham, a director of the club, Matt Gillies and Bert Johnson. The next day (20 January 1962) the team played at Everton, travelling by bus, where I was introduced to the players. I sat in the dugout at Goodison and in all honesty was mesmerised by the atmosphere of over 30,000 supporters, with a toffee lady dressed up in the blue and white of Everton tossing sweets into the crowd.

After the match I had to wait in Liverpool to catch the overnight train back to Edinburgh so one of the Everton players, Bobby Collins, who I knew from my time in Scotland, invited me to his house for tea. Wee Bobby was smaller than me and when I got into his car I noticed he could hardly look over the steering wheel! He always called into the same pub on the way home after a match for a couple of drinks to unwind. My dad always told me, 'Great players don't smoke or drink,' but there weren't many during my career that didn't. He was also celebrating a 3-2 win, scoring Everton's first goal, so I couldn't blame him. Later we went to the Tiger Club, which was frequented by many of the Everton and Liverpool players. When I told him that Leicester City wanted to sign me, Bobby remarked, 'I think you will be okay there Davie, they seem like a nice football club. I'll give you one bit of advice. When you're going well and it's time to sign a new contract, keep the gun at their bloody head. Get the best deal possible, as one day when you're not any good, you'll be out the door!'

It was an unusual bit of advice but Bobby proved to be a good judge. Likewise the perceptive Bert Johnson, as Mike, or 'Stringy' as we all came to know him, and I forged a remarkable double act. Under the guidance of Matt Gillies, the Foxes had consolidated their position in the First Division. Matt was merely looking to refine the blueprint with our signings. My job was to find Stringy, thread the ball wide to him and his pace and strength would do the rest. Howard Riley would provide the balance on the right side to great effect.

The fee was £25,000 and my contract was the same princely sum of £17 a week I was earning at Hibs. It didn't cross my mind to ask for a higher wage at my new club. There were no agents in those days – I was just happy to be given the chance to play in the First Division. I did receive a benefit during my time at Hibernian of about £500 but had to almost crawl for it. I chased them for weeks as I wasn't getting anywhere with Harry Swan, who was an awkward bugger and seldom inclined to loosen the purse strings. In the end I took with me to Easter Road an old friend called Jimmy Sievewright, who was a civil servant and also a freemason. As two businessmen they promptly shook hands and I was paid, although there was nothing put in writing. By way of a footnote, Pat Quinn signed and did well at Blackpool for a while before returning to Scotland in 1963. Who did he sign for? Hibernian.

My first game for Leicester was a friendly against Rotherham, but for my competitive debut I replaced Albert Cheesebrough in a 4-1 home victory against Fulham on 3 February 1962 at Filbert Street. It was also Stringy's home debut – he had taken over from Gordon Wills and latterly John Mitten. I don't remember much about the game other than being so excited. I was rarely used to playing in front of more than 20,000 in Scotland, but attendances far in excess of that were going to be the norm. Jimmy Walsh scored twice, plus one from Ken Keyworth, and a Howard Riley penalty completed a very satisfying afternoon.

Leicester: Banks, Chalmers, McLintock, Norman, King, Appleton, Stringfellow, Riley, Walsh, Keyworth, Gibson.

My home debut for Leicester against Fulham in February 1962. I'm on hand (right) in case keeper Tony Macedo slips up.

The next home match was a 2-2 draw with West Ham – their manager Ron Greenwood generously commented, 'Gibson is going to be one of the big characters in the game.'

I was still doing my stint in the Army and travelled down on the night train from Edinburgh to Leicester via Birmingham on a Wednesday, trained on Thursday and Friday and played on Saturday. Coincidentally, I shared a carriage one night with big Jock Wallace, the West Brom goalkeeper, who was also in the K.O.S.B. before me. He was sleeping in the bottom bunk and his first words to me were, 'Get your little arse upstairs!' I met up with Jock again years later when he took over as manager at Leicester.

At the time there was talk of undertaking an additional six months of National Service after the standard two years if you were based in the UK, so I returned to Aden for a while. I tried to avoid going back again – I kept getting a doctor's certificate even though there was nothing wrong with me. I got away with it for a month until the Army officials sussed me out. I was only in Aden for about a month when a welcome telegram arrived at headquarters. I was required to play for the British Army team, who were undertaking a tour of Hong Kong and Singapore.

Towards the end of May 1962 I flew from Aden to Hong Kong via Gan and Singapore and was on the move for eighteen hours. Everyone complimented me on my tan when I arrived, but I told the lads to be careful when we headed for the beach, as the sun was obviously more severe than back home. I was rooming with my pal Johnny Quinn, who went on to make a name for himself at Sheffield Wednesday. Poor old John – I remember him lying in bed at night covered in calamine lotion to cool his skin down. He was in so much agony from sunburn he couldn't play football for a week.

We had a marvellous tour, winning nine out of ten matches and visiting Hong Kong, Bangkok, Saigon, Kuala Lumpur, Penang and Singapore. In addition to John, the squad included Mick Kearns of Coventry, John Sydenham of Southampton, Bill Baxter of Ipswich, Ken Hale of Newcastle, Mel Scott of Chelsea and the incomparable Jim Baxter of Glasgow Rangers. In the first match against All Hong Kong we were 7-2 ahead when, according to one report,

> The Gibson-Baxter mutual assistance act produced another lovely goal by the inside-right and with two minutes left it was Gibson again. This time he pushed a perfect pass from Baxter through to Quinn. The winger sent it streaking into the net from a narrow angle any soldier could be proud of but it was a bitter pill for Hong Kong.

Another headline was 'Atomic Army blasts Hong Kong. Generals Gibson and Baxter lead the forces to a great 9-2 victory.'

In the second game we beat National China 4-2. It was a scrappy contest and at one stage the crowd expressed their discontent by bombarding us with oranges. Typically Jim Baxter picked one up and calmly peeled it – I thought he'd get us into more trouble! In Kuala Lumpur we stayed at the New Merlin Hotel, a magnificent building and the plushest hotel I had ever seen. We suffered our only defeat there against All Malaya, on the finest soccer pitch I'd played on. Our spirits were lifted in the evening when Rita Hayworth came in for dinner. A few of the lads fancied doing their Frank Sinatra impressions, but thankfully let it pass. I always wish I could have plucked up the courage to ask her for the next dance, even if she probably would have said 'No!' She was sitting at the next table with Gary Merrill, an American film star who she dated for about three years. Leslie Hutchinson, known as 'Hutch', a big cabaret star from the 1920s and 30s, was performing at the hotel. He was a big, handsome lad from Grenada and I remember walking through the swing doors into the lounge when he came through. He nearly knocked me flying – a giant against me at 5 feet 6 inches. 'Sorry my child,' he cried at me.

I firmly believe that six weeks made me as a person and as a professional. As previously mentioned, I'd always suffered from low self-esteem and was never confident of making it as a pro. Some of Jim Baxter's arrogance rubbed off on me – he had enough for everyone on that tour and playing alongside him changed my approach. I never looked back after that and was ready to play against anyone or any team.

On conclusion of the tour I returned to Aden for a few weeks prior to being demobbed. As explained earlier, we had to be up daily at 4.30 a.m. for parade because of the extreme heat. I thought that with so little time before my demob I'd relax and stay in bed. It wasn't long before the sergeant came in with his corporal and put me

My Army team-mate and great friend John Quinn, who made a name for himself at Sheffield Wednesday. If he'd played as well as he looked, he would have been a world-beater.

The British Army team that toured the Far East in 1962. Among the team are, back row: Mick Kearns (Coventry) fifth left, Danny Ferguson (Hearts) eighth, John Gilchrist (Millwall) ninth. Front row: Mel Scott (Chelsea), Pat O'Connor (Kilmarnock), Jim Baxter (Rangers), John Sydenham (Southampton), myself, Bill Baxter (Ipswich), Ken Hale (Newcastle United), John Quinn (Sheffield Wednesday).

right in no uncertain terms. I was put on a charge and did 'jankers' for about five days. I was assigned to peeling potatoes and sweeping sand outside the mess. Every evening we also had to get dressed up for parade, which to be honest was worse than sweeping the sand. It certainly instilled in you a level of discipline that I've never forgotten.

To the tune of 'Will ye no come back again', five young Scots finally marched out of Waterloo Barracks in Aden at the end of July 1962. One of our group was fellow pro Tom White, who returned to play for Raith Rovers. We were the last National Servicemen of the Regiment to leave the K.O.S.B. and the new season couldn't come quickly enough.

I first met Frank McLintock in January 1962 at the Everton match mentioned earlier. From that simple handshake Frank turned out to be the big brother I never had, on and off the pitch. The club found me digs in Avebury Avenue, Leicester with Frank and Billy McDerment, like Frank another Glasgow boy. Billy was about the only footballer I knew who didn't take a drink. He was a lovely lad who drank Coca Cola all night when we went out. Our landlady Mrs Cartwright looked after us brilliantly. She cooked us traditional English food – there were no special diets in those days, although I was given sherry and eggs once to try and build me up. I always felt having a football brain was more important than what you ate.

In the garden of my digs at Avebury Avenue, Leicester, where Mrs Cartwright looked after us.

Mr Cartwright, who must have been seventy-five years old, wanted to sell his car for about £450. Even though I hadn't yet passed my test, I took the plunge and became the proud owner of my first car, a Ford Anglia. Its number was the only one of all the cars I've owned I ever remember – 'WAY 210'. As Frank had already passed, 'L'-plates were fitted and I drove him back and forth to Filbert Street. I was a bit wary of driving through the gate posts to our digs so, as we lived halfway up the hill, I would stop the car and let Frank take over to park the car. After a couple of weeks Frank said, 'Okay, it's about time you parked the car yourself.' I still felt it was too narrow a gap for me to drive through the gates. 'Now take it slowly,' said Frank. Very slowly I crossed the road towards the posts and CRASH! 'I told you it was too f***g narrow,' I shouted at Frank. The front light of my beautiful new car was smashed. Needless to say Frank reverted to parking the car for me.

Whenever the opposition kicked me on the pitch, Frank was right in their face with the threat, 'Do that again and you will have me to contend with.' Not too many kicked me twice. I remember an incident at Everton when another rough, tough and aggressive Scotsman, Jimmy Gabriel, squared up to Frank on the halfway line. Heated words were thrown at each other when Jimmy said, 'O.K. Frank, our team fights your team in the gym after the match.' I quickly looked around the field to see who I was likely to fight. About the only other player of my height and weight was yet another Scot, Alex Young, but Frank had the last word. 'O.K. Jimmy but it's you against me son.' Like most arguments on the field with the adrenalin pumping and emotions high, when the final whistle blew it was soon forgotten and handshakes not fists were the order of the day.

I scored my first goal for the Foxes during the 1-1 draw at Wolves in March 1962. It came from a defensive mix-up, but it was a mixed afternoon for me when a stray pass led to their equaliser. Both sides were comfortably placed in mid-table and, as one of the nationals reported, 'There was only the bonus at stake. And what is £4 to soccer's newly rich these days.' How times change! Stringy and I played together five times towards the end of the season, but it was the following year we started to click with dramatic effect.

7

The Ice Kings

Leicester City had for many years lived under the cheap sneer that it was a somewhat unfashionable club, with no glitter, personalities or big names. Even allowing for the indisputable fact that the Foxes had been a First Division side since 1957, they found it difficult to shrug off an undeserved reputation for being ever so slightly dull. I believe we managed to put that accusation firmly to bed – the marvellous 1962/63 season was our coming of age. We did get off to an inauspicious start in the first game with a 2-1 defeat at Fulham. Who scored both their goals? None other than the team-mate who consoled me in the dressing room after that disastrous Scottish trial match – Graham Leggat. The press reports were more positive: 'Venturing one prediction from this barren battle, I hazard that one full season in English football will see Davie Gibson a perky package of crash, dash and craft in the Denis Law mould, rated in the £50,000+ bracket. A month ago they piped Gibson off an Aden parade ground on his Army release. Let's hope they will not be piping him off to Italy next year as a soccer export.'

Stringy was soon off the mark with six goals from the opening four fixtures as we swiftly rose to a challenging position in the First Division. I also began scoring regularly and even managed a brace at Wolves in a 3-1 victory on 1 December 1962. The first goal resulted from some neat interplay with Jimmy Walsh and Howard Riley before I slipped it into the net. Shortly before half-time Colin Appleton fed me a beautiful ball for the second, which I managed to volley between two defenders. If we took Molineux by storm that day, it was nothing compared to the blizzards that were to sweep the country within a few weeks.

We managed to squeeze in a 5-1 League drubbing of Leyton Orient on Boxing Day, leaving us handily in third place behind Everton and Spurs, before the beginning of the most severe winter in living memory. The 'Big Freeze' had taken its icy grip with ferocious cold and bitter winds. By mid-January temperatures had plummeted to -16C, blocking roads and railways and covering the sea with a solid ice sheet. We couldn't get anywhere near Filbert Street, so Matt Gillies' training sessions were indoors at Granby Halls before he took us for a while to the marginally warmer South Coast and our regular haunt of Brighton. One of the most noticeable

Mike Stringfellow is challenged by Jim Langley in the box at Fulham, a League match in August 1962. I'm number 10 on the right.

Crossing with my right foot against Sheffield Wednesday, August 1962. Tom McAnearney is attempting to intercept.

Foiled by Wednesday's Don Megson and keeper Ron Springett in the same match.

At Highbury in September 1962, as Ian McKechnie dives at my feet in a 1-1 draw against Arsenal, with Terry Neill closing in.

A simple tap-in for the third goal of a 3-0 victory against Liverpool at Filbert Street in October 1962. Jim Furnell is the keeper looking on helplessly.

consequences of the brutal conditions was the enormous disruption to the sporting calendar. Hundreds of football fixtures were postponed and the pools companies, desperate to preserve their takings, having been forced to void their coupons for three successive weeks, inaugurated the Pools Panel to keep their income flowing.

Likewise, clubs were more dependent on gate receipts than nowadays, so many resorted to unorthodox and desperate measures in an effort to thaw out the frozen pitches. Blackpool employed the Army to melt the ice on Bloomfield Road with flamethrowers. Chelsea tried motorway tar burners. During the summer of 1962 Filbert Street groundsman Bill Taylor had relaid the pitch at the suggestion of Alf Pallett, one of the directors, treating the topsoil with a blend of fertiliser and weedkiller. It contained a warming ingredient that reacted chemically in icy conditions to thaw out the surface, which provided a short-term solution to the freeze. However, it was also salt-based, which led to long-term problems with the pitch. Once the snow had been cleared with help from Foxes fans, Bill covered the grass with straw and sat up all night feeding coke into a dozen burning braziers scattered across the pitch. As a result of Bill's efforts, we were back playing at Filbert Street on 9 February, a 2-0 League

January 1963, training at Filbert Street in the snow with Howard Riley.

First game after the 'Big Freeze' – home against Arsenal in February 1963 as I make contact, with Jimmy Magill looking on.

victory over Arsenal. We'd been out of League action for about five weeks; some clubs waited up to ten weeks to resume playing.

We started to play a more direct style of football, taking into account the poor state of the pitches, pinging long passes out wide to Stringy or Howard Riley, which paid dividends. Everton, Nottingham Forest, and Ipswich were dispatched in February to lift us to second place, level on points with Spurs, although the chasing pack had games in hand. We were popularly acclaimed as the 'Ice Kings' or the 'Ice Age Champs' and, with arguably the best Foxes side in living memory also enjoying a decent Cup run, the 'Double' looked a genuinely tantalising prospect.

At the beginning of March 1963 we silenced the Kop with a superb 2-0 victory at Liverpool to maintain our League position. A disciplined performance reaped goals from Ken Keyworth and myself in front of watching Scotland manager Ian McColl. We raised the pulses with great technical, fluid football and Matt encouraged me to push forward and I was scoring regularly. Ken popped up at right half and even full-back, Stringy played centrally as well as wide, Frank McLintock glided forward and Graham Cross dropped back from inside right to a second centre half.

It was our eighth successive victory and the press reports were effusive in praising our style of play. Alan Hoby of the *Sunday Express* described us as 'The Magicians from the Midlands – the greatest Brains Trust in English football'. Sam Leitch in the *Daily Express* was no less gushing – 'The £65,000 heroes of Leicester City unleashed ninety of the most superb and original soccer minutes I have ever seen.

It is a privilege to have watched such technical mastery and disciplined team work.'
Sportsmail reported,

> After all the post-war years of humiliation by crack Continental teams, an English club
> has evolved a technique to match the slick, unorthodox, pattern play of Real Madrid,
> Benfica and Santos. Leicester are producing the most advanced football method to hit
> British soccer in three decades. If their astonishing success run continues they could
> well make as revolutionary a change in British football as Herbert Chapman's third-
> back experiment did in the 1920s.

Praise indeed.

To the eternal credit of the Liverpool players, they actually clapped us off the pitch
and Bill Shankly paid me one of my greatest compliments: 'I haven't seen better inside
forward play for a long time than Gibson produced against us. This boy is certain to
play for Scotland one day and I say that knowing brilliant men like Law and White are
in the Scottish team. Gibson reminds me of the great Wilf Mannion.'

Liverpool: Lawrence, Moran, Byrne, Yeats, Callaghan, Melia, Stevenson, Milne,
Hunt, St. John, Lewis.

Leicester: Banks, Sjoberg, Cross, McLintock, Norman, King, Appleton, Stringfellow,
Riley, Keyworth, Gibson.

A week later we secured another 2-0 win, this time at home to Blackburn. We'd
achieved ten successive wins in League and Cup, setting a club record. The games
were coming thick and fast, and unsurprisingly we looked somewhat jaded during the
early stages of the Manchester United match at Old Trafford on 15 April 1963. Had
the gruelling season finally caught up on us? A late rally with strikes from Graham
Cross and Richie Norman saw us come away with a valuable point in a 2-2 draw. The
following night we somehow summoned the energy in the return fixture to produce
our most memorable League performance of the season. The gates were closed with
37,000 squeezed into Filbert Street, plus a couple of hundred brave fans desperate
to witness the drama perched on the roof. I started the game out wide as Stringy
was injured and Terry Heath came in. Our first goal was scored by Terry, only to be
cancelled out by Denis Law, who at half-time said to me, 'I'd be better in ma bed.'
Twenty minutes later I wished he were after two more strikes to complete his hat-trick,
including a magnificent scissorkick. However, Ken Keyworth matched Law with three
goals in the space of six minutes, all from crosses by Howard Riley at the Filbert Street
end. I became more involved when I moved inside in a pulsating match and our 4-3
victory took us to the top of the League with just five games left.

We were level on points with Everton after a 1-1 draw with Wolves four days later,
but that was as good as it got. We'd played all our home games during the winter, were
left with four away games and lost them all. With a small squad, injuries to Gordon
Banks, Ken Keyworth and Ian King disrupted a settled side. I also picked up an injury
and missed the last three games. We occasionally trained on the Filbert Street car park,
which was covered in ash and had a bit of give in it when you were running about.

The club decided to improve it by surfacing it with tarmac, which looked brilliant. Unfortunately when I went to run, my trainers stopped in the tarmac and I damaged the ligaments in my ankle.

The 'Ice Kings' challenge melted away and, although fourth place was our best in the League since 1928/29, there was intense disappointment for what might have been. We lost our momentum while Everton had a great run-in to take the title. Perhaps the ability to resume playing before other clubs were able to backfired on us in the end. We were having a great spell then, but maybe by the end of the season it had caught up on us. Some people said we also took our foot off the pedal because of the Cup run, but I don't subscribe to that theory. You go out to play football and give it your best. If you lost it was because the other team performed better. I can't think of any of the guys not giving their best. Our main concern was trying to prevent that loss of form carrying into the Cup final...

8

The Road to Wembley

Leicester City's attempt to win the 1961 FA Cup was ruined when Len Chalmers was injured and forced to move from full-back to hobble about on the wing. Tottenham Hotspur showed no mercy in a 2-0 victory. For the seven Foxes survivors, there was renewed optimism that another final was feasible by dint of the form we showed during the first half of the 1962/63 season. Our run started with a visit to Second Division Grimsby Town, never an easy place to go to. The original match was scheduled for the Saturday but called off because of the weather – no League games were contested during January and the third round itself took sixty-six days to complete. We played two days later in the evening of 8 January 1963, on a pitch that more resembled an ice rink. The surface was like granite and we were very surprised the pitch officials passed it fit to play.

Bert Johnson conducted his usual team talk before the match and kept on for ages about Grimsby's Don Donovan, a veteran right back at thirty-four. The whole teamtalk seemed to focus on him – 'Give the ball to Stringy and he'll run at this fella.' At the end Bert asked if anyone had anything to say – nothing. As we walked out of the dressing room Stringy told me he'd already played against Donovan at Mansfield. I said to him, 'Why didn't you speak up, we could have finished Bert's team talk an hour ago!' Perhaps that's an illustration of how much players listen to team talks.

Fortunately we adapted to the conditions quicker than Grimsby. I managed to run onto a Stringy pass and put us one up after just thirty seconds. Ken Keyworth notched a second after my initial shot was blocked, before Grimsby pulled a goal back with a penalty. Nine minutes from time I finished with a side-foot from close range thanks to a terrific low cross from Stringy. Grimsby made a fight of it but failed to penetrate our stubborn defence.

I recall taking a knock near the byline in the second half. With the Grimsby supporters yelling for all they were worth, the referee tried to lift me off the pitch. Our trainer Alex Dowdells was furious with him. 'Don't you touch any of my players while they are on the ground injured.' We actually stayed overnight in Grimsby at the same hotel as the referee. In the morning he came down to breakfast complaining of a bad back. 'Serves you right,' said Alex less than sympathetically, 'for trying to lift my player off the pitch!'

The fourth round against Ipswich Town on 30 January was again played in midweek after being postponed from the previous Saturday. The Filbert Street pitch hardened so quickly in the frost that patches of water became icy and some of the lads had to change their boots. Ipswich took a lead after twenty-eight minutes through Blackwood, but Graham Cross equalised within a minute and Ken Keyworth put us ahead five minutes from the break. With 26,000 roaring us on, Ken swept home Frank McLintock's pass on seventy-seven minutes to seal our passage into the last sixteen.

East London was our next destination in the fifth round against Leyton Orient on 16 March. It was a very tough game, with a gutsy performance from Orient and an inspired display from Gordon Banks. Six minutes from time Howard Riley's pace took him clear on the right and his pinpoint cross was brilliantly met by Ken Keyworth for the only goal.

The sixth-round draw threw up another away tie, this time at Norwich City on 30 March, and Banksie led us out to mark his first cap for England. Norwich put us under a lot of pressure in the first half, but lacked penetration. We made the perfect start after the break when Howard Riley found Stringy with a cross from the right – his flying header did the rest. Twelve minutes later I found some space on the edge of the box and managed to guide the ball inside the far post with my right foot. It was another superb defensive performance, particularly from Graham Cross and inevitably Gordon Banks. One back-breaking save from a rising shot by Tommy Bryceland was the pick. Their star forward was Terry Allcock, who fortunately for us had an off day – he even missed a penalty late in the game.

We were drawn against Liverpool in the semi, played at Hillsborough, Sheffield on 27 April 1963. Under Bill Shankly the Reds had taken the Second Division by storm the previous season and were emerging as a potent force. Players like Jimmy Melia, Ronnie Yeats, Ian St John and Roger Hunt combined to make them a formidable unit, although Melia was injured for this game. We executed a professional mugging that day and I have always compared the tie with the Battle of the Alamo. Our defence was again magnificent, although I will never know how we managed to win. Gordon Banks played the game of his life and was called upon to make more than thirty saves, one from St John in injury time that Frank McLintock reckons was on a par with the famous Pele save. The only goal came from one of our breaks from defence. A wonderful cross on eighteen minutes to the far post from a Howard Riley free-kick was matched by a magnificent jump and header by Mike Stringfellow. I think it was Stringy's best-ever goal for us and he had only just returned from injury. Later on it should have been 2-0 – Stringy came in from the left and I was in the box screaming for him to pull it back, but he shot and missed. I said to him, 'You greedy bastard!' It was one of the few occasions where we weren't on the same wavelength. We rode our luck throughout – Roger Hunt hit the bar and for eighty minutes it was backs to the wall. But what a feeling when the ref blew the whistle to end the match. In that moment we realised we were in the final of the FA Cup, a feeling every footballer deserves to taste. That taste lasted a month before I came down to earth with a huge thud.

Leicester: Banks, Sjoberg, Cross, McLintock, Norman, King, Appleton, Stringfellow, Riley, Keyworth, Gibson.

A spectacular effort in the fifth round of the FA Cup against Leyton Orient in 1963.

Scoring the second goal past keeper Sandy Kennon in the quarter-final of the FA Cup at Norwich in March 1963. I'm the one on the ground.

Mike Stringfellow brilliantly heads the only goal in the FA Cup semi-final against Liverpool.

Liverpool: Lawrence, Lawler, Moran, Byrne, Yeats, Callaghan, Stevenson, Milne, Hunt, St John, Lewis.

Saturday 25 May 1963 is a date I will never forget. It was the weekend of the Monaco Grand Prix, which Graham Hill won for the first time to fulfil his dreams. Would my own 'Voyage of Dreams' become a reality? We were up against Manchester United in the latest Cup final on record, because of the 'Big Freeze'. Wembley Stadium was fully roofed for the first time and looked magnificent. The Foxes fans were in good voice and all seemed set for a classic final. I'd won my first Scotland cap a couple of weeks before and felt fit and confident going into the day. There was certainly no truth in one report I read years later that any of the four previously injured missed some of the League games towards the end of the season to ensure they were fit for the final. Despite our slip-up in the League we remained firm favourites. United had struggled in the League all season and only just escaped relegation. They were, however, not to be underestimated, with some brilliant individuals that Matt Busby was seeking to mould into a team, in many ways the opposite to us. In the event those individuals outplayed us on the day to win 3-1.

I still have nightmares about United's opening goal on the half-hour. Gordon Banks made a great save from Bobby Charlton and, as he always did, looked for and threw it to me. Paddy Crerand, United's brilliant wing half, quickly anticipated what was on. As I tried to trap the ball, it hit my knee and before I could recover Paddy won it and crossed to Denis Law, who demonstrated with his clinical finish that you could never afford him an inch of space. That was the worst I ever felt on a football field. If that wasn't bad enough, replays of past finals are shown every year on Cup final day. More than once my kids have told me I've been trying to trap the ball for fifty years and I still miss it! I always say to them, 'When things are going your way, enjoy every moment, as sooner or later the wheel goes around.' Well my wheel certainly came around on Cup final day.

What an occasion for my form to desert me – it was probably my worst game for Leicester City. In the second half I played a bit deeper to try and create some space, but don't think I passed the ball to Stringy twice. David Herd put them two up after fifty-seven minutes and we were chasing the game. Without doubt it was the biggest disappointment in my football career, not just losing, but the match passed me by. By the end I was gutted and devastated. Perhaps Matt Busby's tactics were that if they stopped me from playing they had a chance, and it certainly worked. As a team maybe we were all trying too hard and, while Ken Keyworth gave us some hope on eighty minutes with a fine diving header, Herd's second five minutes later ended our brief revival and it wasn't to be. As I walked disconsolately off the pitch, referee Ken Aston said to me, 'Cheer up lad. At least you have a chance to return here. I'm retiring now, so that's my lot.' At least he had a decent game and went out on a high.

When I woke up on Sunday morning at the Dorchester Hotel, the first thought that came into my mind was I had missed it, the biggest day in my football career. We travelled back by train a couple of days later and when we got onto the bus in Leicester to take us to the Town Hall, the streets were lined with thousands of supporters

Leicester City's 1963 FA Cup final squad. I'm at the top of the pyramid. Back row: Len Chalmers, Jimmy Walsh, Graham Cross. Middle row: Ian King, Richie Norman, Gordon Banks, Mike Stringfellow, Frank McLintock. Front row: Howard Riley, Ken Keyworth, Colin Appleton, John Sjoberg, Albert Cheesebrough.

Ken Keyworth scores our consolation goal in the 3-1 defeat at Wembley in 1963.

Colin Appleton and I with one of the directors' wives at the evening reception following the FA Cup final. I'm forcing a smile to hide my disappointment.

cheering us. It was the nearest I came to crying as we made our way to a special dinner in the Lord Mayor's Rooms. Even allowing for the 1955 claret and a 1961 Riesling to wash down the dessert of 'Bombe Surprise Filbert', it was hardly the celebration we anticipated.

Over the years supporters have asked me what it felt like to play at Wembley Stadium. I give the reasons on my feelings and they all say, 'But you played there, thousands of young men never get the chance.' I can occasionally look back, dismiss that day and enjoy the magic of the many other good days, but after fifty years it still hurts!

Leicester: Banks, Sjoberg, Norman, McLintock, King, Appleton, Riley, Cross, Keyworth, Gibson, Stringfellow.

Manchester United: Gaskell, Dunne, Cantwell, Crerand, Foulkes, Setters, Quixall, Giles, Herd, Law, Charlton.

The narrative of domestic football throughout the 1960s is understandably dominated by the victors – Liverpool, Manchester United, Manchester City, Leeds and Spurs, with a nod to Burnley and Ipswich. We had been genuine contenders all season for the 'Double', playing stylish football, yet outside Leicester the 'Ice Kings' are now seldom mentioned and largely forgotten. Remarkably, however, we were soon able to bounce back in historic fashion from the disappointment of what might have been.

9

League Cup Success

Having been so close to winning my first honours in domestic football, I felt it important to build on the success of the season and bring one or two new players in. We already had a nucleus of Scottish players in the squad, a deliberate policy by Matt Gillies, and he added to the complement with the signing of Bobby Roberts in September 1963. Of course I'd known Bobby since we were teenagers and I was delighted. Matt would always talk to you about potential new signings, but wanted more than 'He's a good player'. I was able to tell him Bobby trained well and was a very good pro. Matt watched him, signed him and with 280-odd appearances he became an excellent servant to Leicester.

In 1963/64 we never scaled the heights of the previous season in the League – perhaps it was a reaction to our disappointing end, perhaps the distraction of the FA Cup. One highlight was the 3-2 victory over Manchester United at Filbert Street in February 1964, some small consolation for the Cup final defeat. A Denis Law flick – who else – into the back of the net from an early corner set the scene for a riveting match. We equalised before half-time when I crossed from the byline for Stringy to finish calmly. Eleven minutes after the break I chipped the ball across for Billy Hodgson to run on to for our second. Billy, who I felt was underrated during his time at the club, headed us in front soon after and we held onto the lead, despite a late flurry and a goal from David Herd. We ended the season in eleventh position, Liverpool won the title and their domination of English football was on its way.

The League Cup was hatched in 1960 as a midweek competition designed to exploit the fact that many English clubs had equipped their grounds with floodlights. Its survival appeared precarious from the outset, as several top-flight clubs refused to take part, and it was eventually secured only on the promise of automatic Inter-Cities Fairs Cup entry to the winners. Latterly, some of the game's powerhouses have treated the matches as experimental, almost aimless diversions, and often fielded absurdly under-strength sides, using them to experiment with youngsters.

Perhaps Matt Gillies was ahead of his time, as he used the League Cup in 1963/64 to blood some of our aspiring players from the youth team. A case in point was Bob Newton, who made his debut and scored in the second-round 2-0 win over Fourth

October 1963. In the box to finish when defeating Blackburn Rovers 4-3, but what happened to keeper Fred Else, second left?

Division Aldershot (after a bye in the first round). Bob was a bit like Stringy – he could run like the wind and I found him easy to play with. Unfortunately I think he later fractured his cheekbone and was out for a long time. He was never the same, playing just three games for City, and eventually became a painter and decorator – such is the fragility of a professional footballer's career.

In the third round we secured a narrow 2-1 victory at Tranmere Rovers, with goals from Bobby Roberts and Billy Hodgson. Gillingham were our next victims at Filbert Street (3-1), setting up a quarter-final meeting at Norwich City. A Howard Riley goal cancelled out a strike from Ron Davies and we met again at Filbert Street. They proved a tough nut to crack and, with the game evenly poised at 1-1 courtesy of another Billy Hodgson goal, Howard Riley settled it in extra-time to send us through to a two-legged semi-final against West Ham.

Games against the Hammers were invariably high-scoring as they were a free-flowing team and the first leg on 5 February 1964 at Filbert Street was no exception. We flew out of the traps with three goals inside the first twenty minutes. It was one of those purple patches you experience when everything goes right and I had a hand in all three goals. Ken Keyworth was allowed acres of space to head us into the lead from my cross on five minutes. I spirited the ball to Bobby Roberts for the second. Then I put Stringy through and, fending off Ken Brown, he took it round Jim Standen and angled in an absolute gem. We knew it would be a tough tie and they came back strongly with goals from Geoff Hurst (two) and Alan Sealey. I managed to put Frank McLintock through for our fourth a few minutes after the break to give us a slender one-goal advantage.

We were under no illusions about the challenge facing us at Upton Park. They had a good record against us, but on the night we prevented them from getting into their stride with goals again from Frank McLintock and Bobby Roberts. It was hugely satisfying to derail West Ham as they tended to beat us. We'd made another Cup final against quality opposition that included Bobby Moore, Geoff Hurst and Johnny Byrne.

Unfortunately League Cup finals were not staged at Wembley until 1967, so we had to be content with playing the two legs against Stoke City at our respective grounds. The first encounter in April 1964 was at their Victoria Ground. In truth we never got into our stride and were outplayed by a wily and experienced Stoke side. Banksie was brilliant as usual, conceding just the once from Keith Bebbington on sixty-two minutes. I'd say it was his second-best game for us after the Liverpool Cup semi-final and Stoke should have scored five or six. I managed to beat my old pal Lawrie Leslie to equalise with an 18-yarder just inside the box after Terry Heath blocked an attempted clearance from Eric Skeels. We even had a chance late on to take a lead to Filbert Street when John Sjoberg came flying through from right-back to within about 25 yards of the goal. I was alongside, willing him to square it to me, as I would be one-on-one with Lawrie. John did what full-backs do and 'blootered' it over the bar. I remember shouting the odds in the dressing room at John at the end, but Matt told me to calm down. He was happy, as we were fortunate to take a 1-1 draw to Filbert Street.

A crowd of over 25,000 generated a wonderful atmosphere in the return leg and we scored the vital first goal in the sixth minute. John Sjoberg lofted a big kick from just inside the Stoke half down the middle and Stringy brushed aside a couple of tackles to slot it home. We had the upper hand and shots poured on target from Howard Riley, Stringy and Tom Sweenie. Calvin Palmer gave us a fright when he struck the top side of the bar with a header before Stoke drew level with a goal from Denis Viollet just after the break.

The tie was evenly poised until a magical moment on seventy minutes, when I scored with a glancing header from a Riley corner to restore our lead. Howard used to hit them over like bombs and I got a flick to the ball at the near post and it flew into the net. Tom Sweenie sent Howard away for the third and, although Stoke put us under a lot of pressure and produced another goal in injury time, we held on for the Foxes' first-ever trophy in senior football.

Of course the competition was not as big as the FA Cup, but we were all chuffed to bits and I am the only player to score in both legs of a League Cup final. It didn't have the prestige of a Wembley final nor was it on television, but we were happy enough. I always thought Filbert Street was a magical place and on that evening the supporters definitely played their part. When it was full the atmosphere was electric. It was also wonderful to have some of our youngsters making their mark. Frank McLintock missed both legs of the final with injury, making it even more of an achievement. Matt Gillies again gave youth its head, bringing in Max Dougan and Terry Heath for the first leg and Tom Sweenie at Filbert Street. Terry Heath was a decent attacking midfielder and, while he only made eight appearances for the Foxes, he also played

Mike Stringfellow scores our first goal past Bobby Irvine during the 3-2 second-leg win that clinched victory over Stoke City in the 1964 League Cup final.

A flying header for the second goal in the final.

Howard Riley coolly finishes for the third against Stoke.

Captain Colin Appleton is presented with the League Cup trophy.

Celebrations in the dressing room with Bert Johnson, Richie Norman, Colin Appleton, Ian King, Matt Gillies, Tom Sweenie, Mr Needham and Eddie Plumley. It was terrific to see Matt and Bert enjoying their success, as they meant so much to me during my time at the club.

in the 4-3 win over Manchester United mentioned earlier. In fact, it was Terry's last game for the club before he moved on via Hull to become a crowd favourite at Scunthorpe.

First leg – Leicester: Banks, Sjoberg, Dougan, Cross, King, Heath, Appleton, Stringfellow, Riley, Keyworth, Gibson.

Stoke: Leslie, Asprey, Allen, Palmer, Kinnell, Skeels, Dobing, Viollet, Ritchie, McIlroy, Bebbington.

Second leg – Leicester: Banks, Sjoberg, Cross, Norman, King, Appleton, Stringfellow, Riley, Keyworth, Sweenie, Gibson.

Stoke: Irvine, Asprey, Allen, Palmer, Kinnell, Skeels, Dobing, Viollet, Ritchie, McIlroy, Bebbington.

Our appetite and enthusiasm for the competition remained undimmed the following season, particularly when the Football League announced the winners would be entered into the Fairs Cup. We made a modest start, struggling to dispose of Peterborough United, Grimsby Town and Crystal Palace in the early rounds. That all changed in round five at Second Division Coventry City in December 1964, where a crowd of 28,000 witnessed a stunning performance from us. An own goal from Coventry skipper George Curtis gave us an early lead. From then on, almost every shot resulted in a goal. Richie Norman, who didn't score too many, managed a couple and was on for a hat-trick when put clean through. In typical full-back fashion and with only keeper Bob Wesson to beat, he blazed wide. Billy Hodgson and Stringy also helped themselves to a brace each and just a single goal from myself saw us home by an extraordinary 8-1 scoreline. I did have some sympathy for my old Army team-mates Ken Hale and Mick Kearns on the night – Coventry were completely overwhelmed.

We met stiff resistance from Plymouth Argyle, another Second Division side, over the two-legged semi-final. To Argyle's credit, despite having a number of injuries in the first tie at Filbert Street in January 1965, manager Malcolm Allison drafted in some young players who ran themselves into the ground. A 25-yard screamer from Johnny Williams put them into a deserved lead on thirty-five minutes. The game ebbed and flowed in the second half until we equalised with an own goal from Williams following a goalmouth melee. Two minutes later Mike Trebilcock, later an FA Cup hero with Everton, pounced on a loose ball to rifle it home. Back we came with a Bobby Roberts strike, then Stringy teed me up on the edge of the box and I struck the ball low into the corner to grab the winner. Three weeks on and we safely negotiated the away tie with a single goal from John Sjoberg, a belter following a Billy Hodgson short corner. A couple of postscripts – in between the two legs we played Plymouth again, this time in the fourth round of the FA Cup, and demolished them 5-0. In the Argyle side was John Newman, who later became my manager at Exeter.

To celebrate our safe passage to the final, after the match we went out for a few drinks with a curfew set at 11 o'clock. Players being players, some, including yours truly and Billy Hodgson, were late returning to the hotel. Matt Gillies had waited up until midnight at the hotel with the directors and knew there were a few who were still absent. On the Thursday we travelled straight to Blackpool on the train for a match on the Saturday (13 February). As we were about to get off the bus from the railway station to enter the Blackpool hotel, Matt said, 'Those that came in before midnight go to this side, all those after midnight to that side.' It was the first time I'd ever seen him angry. In the morning, David Jones took training for the guys that came in before midnight and Matt took five or six of us. He'd never taken us training and ran the balls off us! He gave us some fearful stick and said if we didn't get a result at Bloomfield Road, we'd all be in trouble. Fortunately we came away with a 1-1 draw with a strike from Jimmy Goodfellow – thanks Jimmy!

The incentive of European competition added an extra dynamic to the final against Chelsea and the first leg in March 1965 at Stamford Bridge was hotly contested. They played with ten men from the thirteenth minute, when Alan Young was injured in a tussle with Gordon Banks. Our tactics were fairly rudimentary once that happened – attack! Unfortunately it left gaps in our defence that Chelsea exploited twice, with goals from Bobby Tambling and a penalty from Terry Venables. We fought back, courtesy of goals from Colin Appleton and Jimmy Goodfellow, and gave no thought of being content to take a draw to Filbert Street. Then disaster struck with ten minutes to go as Chelsea gained the upper hand with a goal that should never have happened. Keeper Peter Bonetti threw the ball out to Eddie McCreadie, he raced up the field and three defenders sought to intervene, Ian King, Len Chalmers and Richie Norman.

Banksie arrived simultaneously, McCreadie stuck out a toe and it bounced four times before trundling into the empty net.

We remained confident of overturning the deficit in front of almost 27,000 fans on 5 April 1965. We laid siege to the Chelsea goal, but their defence held firm and Peter Bonetti was in inspired form. For all our concerted efforts to break Chelsea down, the leg ended goalless. In fairness they had some very good players – Bobby Tambling was a goalscorer and a half – but we should have beaten them. They also defended well: I remember John Boyle ran into me and I felt that – he was a tough Scot.

First leg – Leicester: Banks, Sjoberg, Norman, Chalmers, King, Appleton, Hodgson, Cross, Goodfellow, Gibson, Sweenie.

Chelsea: Bonetti, Harris, McCreadie, Hinton, Young, Hollins, Boyle, Venables, Murray, Tambling, Graham.

Second leg – Leicester: Banks, Walker, Norman, Roberts, Sjoberg, Appleton, Hodgson, Cross, Goodfellow, Gibson, Stringfellow.

Chelsea: Bonetti, Harris, McCreadie, Mortimore, Hinton, Boyle, Venables, Upton, Murray, Tambling, Bridges.

Peter Bonetti dives to save for Chelsea in the second leg at Filbert Street of the 1965 League Cup final.

10

The Foxes Hunt More Glory

After an encouraging start, our form ebbed and flowed in the League and the final position of eighteenth was a disappointment. We enjoyed a 'double' over Liverpool, I scored in a 4-2 home win over Spurs in October 1964 and Fulham were beaten 5-1 in February 1965, Jimmy Goodfellow scoring a hat-trick, but we lacked consistency.

The 3-2 defeat at Leeds in September 1964 was memorable for me, as it was the only time in my career I was sent off. Not for dangerous play but for dangerous swearing. I admired Leeds for their ability to play, but I never admired their ability to intimidate the opposition and the referee. I'm certain over the years this was the principal reason they were never liked or spoken about with the same sincerity as, for example, Spurs or Burnley in their prime. This day was no exception – they were as attritional as ever. Early on, Colin Appleton tackled wee Billy Bremner on the edge of the penalty box, right on the byline. He slid in and got the ball, but Billy dived and went flying onto the track. That marked my first swearing session at the ref, as he gave a penalty. Bremner scored the penalty himself, his second of the match, but we responded well with goals from Tom Sweenie and Howard Riley to level at 2-2. Then Albert Johanneson, their left-winger, made it 3-2, albeit from an offside position. With a few minutes to go Graham Cross drove forward and hit a gem of a strike into the top corner to equalise from about 30 yards; we'd got our just rewards. We were running back to the half-way line celebrating the goal when Billy and all the other Leeds players surrounded the ref, pointing to the linesman, who had his flag up. 'Who the hell was offside?' I enquired. Can you believe they gave Howard Riley off, even though he was yards away out on the right wing. We couldn't believe it. How was Howard interfering with play so far wide? Sadly I lost the plot – I couldn't stop swearing and dived into Johnny Giles. He gave another foul, I called him a 'f***g cheat' and was sent off. I felt we had a raw deal from him all the match. An interesting fact for the statisticians is that on that day in 1964 a record number of six players were sent off in the League, but I bet I was the only one sent off for swearing!

Over the years Leeds won many trophies but not too many friends. They could have won more, but I honestly feel the Gods deserted them and they got their comeuppance. The FA Cup defeat to Chelsea in 1970 and losing to Wolves in the last League game of

Fame at last as I make it into a cigarette card series.

1972, which enabled Derby to snatch the title from them, spring to mind. They were excellent footballers who didn't need to intimidate – they certainly should have won many more trophies. Billy Bremner, John Giles and Norman Hunter were outstanding footballers but they didn't think twice of kicking the shit out of you, especially if you were playing well. Worse than that trio were the two on the bench, Don Revie and his sidekick Les Cocker, who took great satisfaction in intimidating the opposition. I remember them shouting, 'Billy, Johnny, Norman, number 10, kill the bastard.'

People tend to associate hard men and Leeds with 'Bites yer Legs' Hunter and Bremner but his team-mate Eric Smith, who was previously at Celtic, was the hardest footballer I played against. He was a stocky wee bald-headed lad, tough and uncompromising, and wing half in the Scottish League team that I was up against in 1959 when selected for Scotland in that fateful friendly. Paddy Clarke from my Winchburgh Works team remembers an Army final in the mid-1950s against Highland Light Infantry (H.L.I.), who had this little guy kicking everybody. Paddy, being a similar type, thought he'd have him. That same Eric Smith came running through and Paddy whacked him. They both fell to the ground but unfortunately for Paddy he landed under Smith, who got up first and stood on every bit of his body. He was getting some practice in before being transferred to Leeds! Paddy was tough but he met his match that day.

John Kurila of Northampton Town, who would kick his grandmother, was another hard man, as was Sheffield Wednesday left-back Don Megson – he had muscles on his muscles. Tony Kay, also of Sheffield Wednesday and then Everton, kicked everybody, especially me. On one occasion when we played Everton I sent Stringy up the left wing then made a run into the box. The next thing I remembered was waking up in the dugout. When I came to I thought I'd fallen over, but had accidentally run into Tony's elbow – his words not mine. He was a very good player but a bit nasty. Then of course there was Tommy Smith – thou shalt not pass...

In the FA Cup we safely negotiated through to the sixth round before Liverpool gained some revenge for the 1963 Cup semi-final with a 1-0 victory after a replay. A Roger Hunt goal at Anfield in March 1965 put paid to our hopes of another semi-final. Marking me that day was former Leicester manager Gordon Milne. The wing half was all over me like a rash – every time I tried to receive a pass, Gordon was there. At half-time Matt Gillies had his team talk and when he got round to me said, 'Davie, you're our playmaker, you make it happen and you're not in the game.' I replied, 'Boss, it's a bit tough out there with Milne over me but leave it with me, I'll sort it out.' Fifteen minutes into the second half, once again he was breathing down the back of my neck. Waiting for the ball to arrive at my feet, I thought emergency action was needed. At the very last moment I gave him an elbow in the solar plexus. All's fair in love and war, so they say, and this was war. I heard the grunt and gasp – that's sorted you out, you little sod. As I looked down in shock and horror, it wasn't Gordon I had belted but Tommy Smith, one of the hardest men in football. Tommy was knelt on one knee gasping, 'Gibson you dirty bastard.' I couldn't really say, 'Sorry Tommy I thought it was Gordon!' He eventually got to his feet and moved towards me pointing his finger. I found the safest place on the field, which was behind the referee. Tommy still came forward: 'See you Gibson, I'm going to break your f***g leg.' 'Did you hear that ref?' I pleaded in desperation. 'I certainly did Davie, but he was talking to you not me,' he replied reassuringly. Thankfully I survived to play another day.

In May 1965 Matt Gillies made two significant signings, Derek Dougan for the bargain price of £21,000 from Peterborough and Jackie Sinclair from Dunfermline for £25,000. They both made their debut in the Foxes' first game of the season, a 3-1 home defeat to Liverpool in August 1965. My first recollection of Derek was back in 1960 when I was on tour with Hibernian. Our opening match was a friendly against Portsmouth. The next day the team had tickets for the FA Cup Final, the first time I had ever been to Wembley. I didn't know any of the English players and wanted Blackburn to beat Wolves, but only because I liked the colour of their shirts. Wolves thrashed them that day, but I recall on the eve of the final Derek asked for a transfer, which must be unique in the game.

In December 1962 Derek played against us for Aston Villa in a 3-3 draw, yours truly scoring twice. He then lost his way for a couple of years and dropped down the leagues to Peterborough. It wasn't until Matt gave him a lifeline that I finally met up with this likeable Irishman. He was a real Jekyll and Hyde, inclined to be lazy, but he led the forward line with unique flair. After those years in the wilderness Derek was starting to mature and showed the kind of form he had earlier displayed at Blackburn and Aston

Villa. Jackie Sinclair was a terrific little goalscoring winger and the two of them hit it off from the start. We had a decent side in 1965/66, could score goals for fun and finished a respectable seventh place in the League.

There were always challenges thrown at us in training. Derek was big and lanky, 6 feet 3 inches, but he seemed to float around the track at Filbert Street. A race was set up once against a young lad called Bob Mackay, a seventeen-year-old who could run a bit. The Doog actually gave him a start from the corner flag to the goal, about thirty yards. The trainer shouted 'Go' and the Doog caught Bob before they reached the goal at the other end of the pitch. He was long legged and deceptively quick, a bit special. There was another exercise in medicine balls and I couldn't believe it when he picked two up and ran a lap round the pitch with one under each arm. I could hardly lift one.

He must have been a manager's nightmare you couldn't leave him out of the team, but you never knew which Doog was going to turn up, and sadly our time together was over all too soon. His reputation caught up with him, rather unfairly in my opinion. We were knocked out of the FA Cup in the third round by Manchester City towards the end of January 1967. That gave us a free weekend three weeks later when the fourth-round ties were played, so Matt took us to Brighton for a few days. On the Saturday we watched Brighton play Chelsea in the Cup and in the evening the lads went out for a drink. Matt wanted us back at the hotel by 11.30 – no problem. Sunday was a free day, so Derek decided to visit an old pal in Portsmouth, Sammy Chapman, who he played with when he first arrived from Ireland. I was rooming with Derek and the following morning, when our trainer David Jones knocked on our door, there was no sign of Derek. I told him where he'd gone and shortly afterwards Derek actually appeared. He explained the weather had been so atrocious he stayed overnight at Sammy's and I honestly believed him. I told him he'd better report to David quick, as he was pretty upset to find he hadn't slept at the hotel. Eventually Derek returned to the room and jokingly I asked him how much he'd been fined. 'Nothing,' said Derek, 'they're sending me home.'

The team bus arrived back in Leicester on the Wednesday afternoon and I found Derek waiting in the car park. Once again I asked him if he'd been fined. This time he said, 'No I've been transferred to Wolves.' To say I was shocked by the news was putting it mildly. I was sad to be losing a good friend and a footballer who, with 41 goals from 76 appearances, demonstrated the talent he really had. What a bonus for Wolves and with hindsight it could have been the start of our decline, leading to relegation in 1969. The following eight seasons were probably the best Derek ever played, scoring an amazing 123 goals in 323 games. Never in my wildest dreams did I think his career would go into orbit. Derek was a loveable rogue who I'm glad I met along the way.

A 5-1 thrashing of Burnley in November 1966 was a match I recall for many reasons, not least as it came two days after I married Mavis; more about that later. We played some brilliant football that day and built up a lead in spectacular fashion. Surprisingly it took us until the fortieth minute to open the scoring, as we had created numerous chances. Derek Dougan's shot was blocked on the line by John Angus, only for Peter Rodrigues to stab the ball home. Jackie Sinclair doubled the lead just before half-time. It was my turn on forty-eight minutes when I latched on to a pass from Jackie.

Leicester's home internationals in our respective kit; Derek Dougan (Northern Ireland), Gordon Banks (England), myself (Scotland) and Peter Rodrigues (Wales).

I was tempted to blast the ball, but seeing Adam Blacklaw off his line decided on a delicate chip instead. It worked to perfection, one of my best ever goals and Jackie and Stringy completed a 5-1 rout. It was probably our most impressive performance of the season, despite a greasy pitch and unpleasant conditions. Our League position was a very respectable fifth at the time and, although we slipped to eighth by the end of the season, we continued to hold our own as a Division One side.

During the 1967/68 campaign we struggled following the departure of Gordon Banks and Derek Dougan. Matt Gillies went out and bought Willie Bell from Leeds, the Charlton winger Len Glover and Northampton forward Frank Large to bolster a squad that included some promising youngsters, including Peter Shilton and David Nish. Our form subsequently picked up and we climbed to the relative safety of thirteenth place by the end of the season.

We enjoyed a decent FA Cup run, the highlight being in February 1968 when we defeated Manchester City 4-3 in the fourth round. How did we beat them, after going 2-0 down? A superb first goal for the club from Rodney Fern seconds from half-time couldn't have come at a better time. However, it was mainly down to the ultimate journeyman Frank Large, who weighed in with two goals to add to a strike from David Nish. Frank's infectious enthusiasm inspired us to score four times in twenty minutes on that day. Frank was a very brave player, keepers crapped themselves when he was about. He was prepared to get cuts, break his nose, he wasn't really a football player but was brave as a lion.

Leicester City 1967/68 squad. Back row: Len Glover, Graham Cross, Frank Large, Mike Stringfellow, Peter Shilton, Peter Rodrigues, Alan Woollett, David Nish, Willie Bell. Front row: John Sjoberg, Jackie Sinclair, Bobby Svarc, Bobby Roberts, Alan Tewley, myself, Richie Norman.

A tussle with Manchester City's Tony Book.

Leicester *v*. Arsenal, I seem to have sent Terry Neill a dummy.

Having seen off Manchester City, we struggled to overcome Tommy Docherty's Rotherham in the next round, but Frank's contribution was again telling in the replay in March 1968. During the first half reserve keeper Colin Mackleworth went 'route one' and, as Frank challenged their goalkeeper Alan Hill to the ball, Hill came out and hit Frank with a right hook. It flattened him and smashed his nose all over his face. Normally that would have been the end of the story, but Frank had treatment and carried on. It must have shaken Hill up too, as when a cross came later on he froze – he didn't fancy it. Frank put it away and Stringy got the other one but it was to no avail, as we disappointingly lost 3-1 in the quarter-finals to Everton.

The 1968/69 season was a very difficult one. We struggled from the outset and by November 1968 the board felt it was time for a change. The directors had a meeting with some of the players including myself, as one or two were not happy with Bert Johnson – not me, I thought the world of him. However when the team is not winning, players will always blame someone. Managers and coaches didn't get dismissed too often back then, but sadly Bert was sacked by the board shortly after. Being the man Matt was, he resigned in protest but kept it from us. The day after we went to Everton and were hammered 7-1. It was a very emotional occasion as Matt told us in the dressing room after the game that he had resigned. It was the first and only time I had ever seen a manager break down when making that fateful resignation to his players. It was the same month Matt had become the first manager to survive ten years in the post and was a very sad day for Leicester City. George Dewis was another casualty, being demoted from the reserves to look after the youth team. Frank O'Farrell was appointed in his place soon after and I was to find out to my cost that his management style was in complete contrast to Matt.

11

Wembley Beckons Once More

We languished at the foot of the League all season but enjoyed another great FA Cup run – how often does that seem to happen? In the early rounds we overcame Barnsley and Millwall with hard-fought ties before drawing Liverpool. After a battling goalless draw at the beginning of March 1969 in front of 42,000 supporters at Filbert Street, two days later nearly 55,000 people packed into Anfield to witness a stunning replay. Against all the odds, we took the lead after thirty-four minutes when Andy Lochhead, who signed in November 1968, outjumped big Ron Yeats from a Len Glover cross to head unerringly home. My personal favourite ever save of the many Peter Shilton made came on thirty-nine minutes, when he dived to his left to save a Tommy Smith thunderbolt penalty. Peter knew Tommy tended to go to the right and practised penalties the previous day. We withstood extreme pressure throughout the second half to seal a memorable victory, and then overcame stubborn Mansfield in the quarter-final with a Rodney Fern winner to be pitted against West Brom in the semi.

I was disappointed to miss out through injury, but we played well at Hillsborough that day and a late goal from Allan Clarke proved just enough to see us through to my second FA Cup final in six years. Brian Madley of *The People* captured the drama:

West Brom started full of confidence. Leicester risked losing midfield supremacy by playing Alan Woollett there instead of the accomplished Nish, who remained in the back four and Albion had so much of the play that it seemed they must go right on top. They let the opportunity slip and a Bobby Hope shot that hit the bar was their only reward. Leicester looked jittery but in Graham Cross, John Sjoberg and nerveless goalkeeper Peter Shilton they had men who looked capable of stopping anything. And when the second half came with the wind in their favour, it was obvious that they had succeeded. City's hopes could have been sunk when Len Glover was taken off with a groin injury twenty-five minutes from the end, but it was an event Leicester had anticipated. The arrival of substitute Malcolm Manley coincided with a period of Leicester dominance that was to prove decisive. They suddenly raised the pace and produced the first signs of nervous tension in the Albion defence. Lochhead niggled away at them all afternoon and their nerves reached breaking point as Nish crossed to

Andy Lochhead's majestic header in the fifth-round replay of the FA Cup at Anfield against Liverpool in March 1969.

1969 FA Cup final squad. Back row: John Sjoberg, Peter Rodrigues, Len Glover, Andy Lochhead, Frank O'Farrell (manager), Malcolm Musgrove (trainer), Graham Cross, Bobby Roberts, Allan Clarke, Mike Stringfellow, Alan Woollett. Front row: Rodney Fern, David Nish, Peter Shilton, myself, Malcolm Manley.

the centre. This time Lochhead was unchallenged and allowed to nod down to Clarke, running in from 25 yards. Clarke took the ball in his stride and, with his right foot, hit it without great power but with killing accuracy.

In our way stood Manchester City, a team packed with attacking potential and brought together by the shrewd Joe Mercer and highly rated coach Malcolm Allison. They had won the League the previous season and this time we were definitely the underdogs. Saturday 26 April 1969 dawned an overcast day but I felt bright, confident and, at thirty, blessed with sufficient maturity to handle the occasion more effectively than last time. I actually had a cortisone injection beforehand in my knee, having missed the semi with a ligament injury. It was the only one I had in my career – I didn't want it, but I was determined to play after my chastening experience in 1963. We played our part in an exciting match, Andy Lochhead missed a couple of golden opportunities to score, but it wasn't our day. We were undone by a superb goal in the first half from Neil Young. Captain Tony Book could have been Man of the Match, Mike Summerbee should have been, but it was awarded to Allan Clarke. Mick Doyle kicked the shit out of me, but then he did that every time we played City. They were the better team and deserved to win, but the defeat was especially hard to take for myself and Graham Cross, the sole survivors from 1963. Graham was probably our best player on the day and we even stuck him up front in desperation to try and grab an equaliser. Someone once said, 'It's not the winning that counts, it's the taking part' I'll go along with that to a point, but what was it with me and Manchester? Years later I came to terms with the defeats when I watched the movie *Gone with the Wind*. Now when I play tennis, snooker or golf and have a bad day, I remember Scarlett O'Hara's words as Clark Gable walks away. 'Tomorrow is another day.' Disappointed, maybe, but I'll be back again tomorrow. In 2009 one of my great friends, Fred Ayre, kindly invited me to City's fortieth anniversary of their Cup final victory. It was only the second time I had been back to Manchester in forty years for two very good reasons.

Leicester: Shilton, Rodrigues, Nish, Woollett, Roberts, Cross, Fern, Gibson, Lochhead, Clarke, Glover. Sub: Manley.

Manchester City: Dowd, Book, Pardoe, Doyle, Booth, Oakes, Summerbee, Bell, Lee, Young, Coleman. Sub: Connor.

After the Cup final we had just five matches to rescue our season. Following two wins and a defeat we came up against Everton at Filbert Street on 14 May 1969. It was always a formidable midfield encounter, with Alan Ball and Colin Harvey very competitive players. I had a personal battle that day with Harvey, who was a decent player. I was never aggressive and football is competitive – you have to get in a tackle if you can. I was trying to play one-twos when I got on the ball and 'whack', in came Harvey. I thought if that's the way you want it, I'm going to have a go at you as well. My personal battle was so intense that Colin lost the plot. In the second half he had a wild kick at me which went somewhere between my knee and my chest! Unfortunately for him it was right next to the dugout and right under the nose of the linesman, who promptly raised his flag. The referee had seen it as well and Colin was sent off. In the

Captain David Nish introduces Allan Clarke to Princess Anne before the 1969 FA Cup final. I'm looking on with Graham Cross.

heat of the moment the Everton players surrounded me *en masse* as I was lying on the ground getting treatment. 'Get up you lazy bastard' was one of the more polite comments. Somehow I managed to steer clear of the ferocious tackles that were coming my way for the rest of the match. I thought after the game that Frank O'Farrell should have told me to play up front in the box, as if they were going to kick me I might as well get a penalty for my troubles. Rodney Fern finally substituted me towards the end of the match and we managed a 1-1 draw.

About ten days later the club received a letter from Everton stating Colin Harvey had appealed against the sending off. Frank asked me if I was prepared to go to the appeal and say a few words on Colin's behalf. I told Frank that if it would help restore some harmony between the two clubs I would consider it. However, I couldn't see the logic in speaking up for someone who might have badly injured me and on reflection declined. Perhaps that didn't endear me to Frank but it struck me as a bizarre request.

Three days later, on the last day of the season, we suffered a 3-2 defeat by Manchester United and were relegated. For the second time in the space of a month I was devastated. I broke down and for the only time in my career cried in the dressing room. It was the saddest day of my career. We actually put up a brave effort but it was always going to be a big ask at Old Trafford. I felt we had let everybody down – I'd never experienced relegation before and it really hit me.

There were several reasons for our poor season. Certainly injuries and loss of form to key players were factors. Allan Clarke was undoubtedly a prolific player, but at the start of the season we paid Fulham big money plus Frank Large for him, only to be relegated – make of that what you want. He was an outstanding goalscorer, but as a personality he wasn't one of the guys. There were a couple of things that put me off. Just before we played Manchester United in that last game, Frank O'Farrell told us, 'Allan says he can't go to Old Trafford, his wife's not well.' She had a cold! When we reached the Cup final John Sjoberg, David Nish and myself were involved in organising the players' pool, where we accumulated any monies received from interviews, adverts, photos etc. Two players didn't want to go into the pool, so they could make money for themselves. I went to David Nish and asked him what we could do. He asked me to have a word with them. Peter Shilton changed his mind and I asked Allan for the last time when we were on the treatment table the week before the final, but he wasn't shifting. A few weeks after the final and after Allan had left for Leeds, we received a letter from him enquiring what his share of the pool was. We let him know none too politely that as he wasn't in the pool he wouldn't get anything.

Unfortunately, the end at Leicester was not the way I would have liked. I always say this wonderful game can turn a manager into a Jekyll and Hyde, and Frank O'Farrell certainly fitted that personality trait. He could be the nicest person in the world before a game and a lunatic afterwards, but I got on okay with him until the end of my Leicester career. I was in and out of the side at the beginning of the 1969/70 season and knew the end was coming, so I asked for a transfer. I was hoping they would let me go on a 'free' so I could try my luck elsewhere, realistically at a lower level. Frank said he would speak to the directors and a week later told me they were not keen to let me go – 'The directors are worried you might go somewhere else and play well!' So I started the season in the reserves and quite enjoyed it, playing with the kids, then after about four weeks Frank called me in on a Monday. 'They've decided to let you go,' he said. Of course, if they had released me during the close season I would have had all summer to try and find a club so it wasn't ideal, but I really wanted to play first team football. I asked if I could still come down and train, not with the first team but with the kids, while I got fixed up with another club. I didn't want to train on my own and not push myself hard enough. Frank's reply shocked me – 'No, I've had enough trouble with you already. When you go out of that door, don't come f***g back.' I don't think I deserved that – I never gave any manager any problem throughout my career and thought those comments were unforgivable. Perhaps I caught him on a bad day…

After nine wonderful years at Leicester, 339 appearances and 53 goals, my last match was at Birmingham in February 1970, when John Farrington scored the only goal. I left with a heavy heart, but so many memories of the special atmosphere at Filbert Street, especially under floodlights with the crowd being so close to you. When I was latterly sub, quite often I didn't bother going in at half-time, as there were more likely than not going to be shouting matches in the dressing room. I tried to entertain the crowd on the pitch with a bit of ball juggling or passing the ball across the half-way line. The idea was for me to meet the ball at the exact moment it arrived on the other side of the pitch. I ran around the 'D' on the half-way line across the pitch and the crowd loved it.

I enjoyed my role as playmaker, although occasionally played wide left-wing or wide right-wing. I didn't mind playing wide later in my career but I was never that fast. Just after the 1966 World Cup, we played Borussia Dortmund at home. In the dressing room Matt Gillies said, 'Who's going to play centre forward?' I volunteered as it was only a friendly and he agreed. They played with a sweeper and every time he came forward to play us offside I went with him. It stumped him so much that he argued with his defenders over who was marking me. I was actually marking him so they couldn't pass it back to him. In the event we won 6-0.

It was a privilege to play with so many quality team-mates. Ian King was more of a footballer than a stopper who just defended. He could have played further forward – he was very tidy with the ball at his feet and was a terrific five-a-side player. He could pass the ball from the back and would comfortably slot into today's style of play.

Colin Appleton was a superb captain and a terrific pro. As the left half he was a good tackler and a winner. He was also the first guy who got me to drive a car. His Morris Minor was in the old car park at Filbert Street when he persuaded me to jump in before I had taken any lessons. I was only going about 5 mph but panicked as I thought I'd run into the railings. I was frightened I wouldn't stop even though I had the whole car park to turn the car!

Wee Howard Riley was a flyer on the right wing with a thunderbolt of a cross – it never came in gently. He was a good dribbler up and down the line and could give fullbacks a roasting. Ken Keyworth was a wing half converted into a centre forward, who scored many important goals for us. He was big and lazy with an easygoing nature and played like that. He wasn't a playmaker but at over 6 feet was a terrific header of the ball. Richie Norman at left back played over 300 times for the club. He had a solid

Leaping a challenge from Chelsea's Eddie McCreadie, a tough Scottish compatriot. John Boyle, another hard Scot, is in the background.

defence, and one of the main reasons for our success as a team was that we didn't give much away at the back. Richie played his part and was unlucky not to win a cap.

Peter Rodrigues and David Nish were two superb full-backs. Peter was very quick and could tackle. I first saw David as a kid at the club at sixteen – he already looked a class act. He started in midfield before being converted to full-back and had an elusive movement about him, a bit like Stanley Matthews. He had a great touch and could find you from 10 or 30 yards. He went on to star at Derby and was a bit special.

Alan Woollett wasn't a class act, but you could put him in a team and he was a good man-marker – he could stop the opposition playing. He wasn't a classic runner but got around the pitch effectively. When John Sjoberg was injured in the FA Cup final Alan came in and didn't let us down. When I started at Leicester, John was right-back and one of those defenders who wasn't overly comfortable on the ball, so it could end up in the stand. But he could defend and that's why he was in the team. When he moved to centre half he became a better player and was magnificent in the air. He was tough as teak, which Blackburn Rovers' centre forward John Byrom discovered when we played them. Byrom was dropping deeper and deeper to get away from John until one of his team-mates shouted, 'Get up the pitch.' Byrom's response was, 'You f***g go and play against him!' John Sjoberg was very dependable – even his knees were hard.

Rodney Fern was an elusive guy who could play anywhere. He won umpteen matches with vital goals and was a bit of an unsung hero. Len Glover was a flamboyant cockney who often stole the headlines. He was the only winger I had to pass the ball back to – he was always behind me as he wandered away from the full-back. Once he got the ball at his feet, though, he was a brilliant runner and dribbler. I called him the 'Ooh Aah' man – when he got the ball and ran at the full-back the crowd went 'Ooh'. Then as he cut inside and shot, it went over the bar and they would go 'Aah!'

I grew up with Bobby Roberts and we played together on Sundays as kids at Gullane. He started his career as a lad on the left wing and went to Motherwell with Billy Hunter. Bobby was a very competitive, aggressive lad and over nearly seven years at Leicester proved to be an excellent signing. He was a similar player and natural successor to Frank McLintock. He could tackle and scored some crucial goals for the Foxes, although Frank was perhaps more of a leader.

And thanks to Matt Gillies and Bert Johnson for also discovering my sidekick Mike Stringfellow, a brave and fast winger. They said I was a good passer of the ball – it was only good when he 'caught' it. I simply had to fizz the ball out to Stringy, or more correctly he didn't want it at his feet, but in front of him while he was racing through the gears. He could cross it or burst through on his own and score. There was almost a mental telepathy between us. I could swap roles with him and play sharp, angled passes into the box for Ken Keyworth or the 'Doog'. One report described our relationship as: 'Gibbo alternatively grafted and ghosted, but always with immaculate perception and pace. Stringy read those threaded passes, lengthening his stride to meet them, and either bulldozing bravely towards goal himself or hitting the byline and whipping in a measured cross.'

Bert would spend ages before a game on the details of the shuttle system between Graham Cross and Frank McLintock, then turned to Stringy and I with the telling throwaway comment, 'Oh and on the left side, you just play your normal game.' Unfortunately Mike suffered a serious cartilage injury at the end of 1968 and lost some of his potency, but we played together in 224 League games and 43 Cup matches. Stringy scored 97 goals in all – not bad for a winger.

It's amazing how Frank and Graham switching positions during a game threw the opposition. Graham was a big strong inside right, Frank was right half, but when Graham moved back for a breather Frank, who had a terrific engine, broke very quickly and it evolved from there. It was back in the days when full-backs marked wingers etc., and seemed to completely confuse teams when they started to interchange. Liverpool copied us and did exactly the same with Tommy Smith and Gordon Milne. It wasn't a master tactical move from Matt or Bert, more an evolving process. Certainly they had studied the great Austria and Hungary teams of the 1950s and encouraged the positional flexibility of our wing halves, inside forwards and wingers. They trusted and encouraged us, and let us get on with it. There's a great saying, 'Play players for what they can do, not what they can't.' I like to think I had a football brain so this desire to give us the freedom to express ourselves certainly suited my game.

Matt and Bert were wartime colleagues at Bolton. It was no great surprise when Matt, who had been appointed manager at Leicester in 1958, invited Bert to the club within a year, albeit originally as head scout. I greatly admired Matt – he was a decent man and apparently might have become a doctor had not football taken such a hold on his life. He was never a coach, though – he left that to Bert. Great managers don't tell players how to play, but they pick the right players and the right team, that's their gift. You could argue he didn't select the right side for the 1961 Cup final when he left Ken Leek out in favour of Hugh McIlmoyle. But it was rumoured that Ken, who was a lovely guy, had gone to a pub with some friends shortly before the final and in the eyes of Matt, a man of principle, he had done something seriously wrong and wholly unprofessional.

Only after I signed for Leicester did I learn that Matt was born in West Calder, just a few miles from Winchburgh. And when he signed as a boy amateur with a Scottish Junior club, it was for Winchburgh. Would you believe my uncle Dick Sneddon was Winchburgh secretary at the time and signed him. He explained once in an interview the background behind my arrival:

> I had always wanted to sign an inside forward of Gibson's type, even before we lost to Spurs at Wembley in 1961. Leicester were the first club to go after John White when he was at Falkirk. We chatted into the early hours with Tommy Younger who was managing Falkirk at that period. But White of course went to Spurs and that was that. Gibson is similar to White in many ways. He pops up where least expected. He's in the right place at the right time and he gets more goals than John does. He has tremendous enthusiasm, is a wonderful fighter and gives a top level performance in every game.
>
> A lot of people thought £25,000 was a lot of money to spend on a player who had been described as a reserve who was going abroad. In any case we really bought him for the following season. Fortunately he had a few games for us before he went off and our supporters liked him. I shall always remember one thing Davie did against Sheffield Wednesday at the start of the season. There he was on the left side of the Wednesday goal. Two defenders were coming at him right across his path. He was hemmed in. Suddenly Davie turned and whipped round the ball, shielding it with his body. Then, with his back to the defenders, he flicked it over his left shoulder and over their heads. Simultaneously, with the crowd gasping, he ran round the right side, collected the ball and crossed it. It all happened in split seconds, it was just like the flick of a coin. The crowd were so stunned it took their breath away. They didn't start to cheer until ten seconds later.

Thanks Matt.

Bert Johnson was a very special person. He never swore, which was almost unheard of in football circles, and never raised his voice in anger. I had a soft spot for Bert because he chose me and shaped my destiny. Whenever we went out of the dressing room he would stop and say, 'Davie, just you go out and play. Get the ball and pass it.' The *Topical Times* annual asked me once if I could do an article on ball control. I sat there and wrote it out. How you would play with a wee tennis ball when you were a kid and spend hours playing keepie-uppey until you were master of the ball. When I

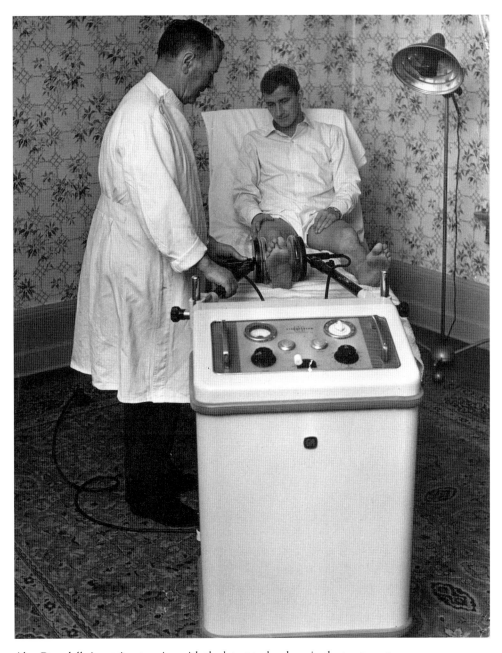

Alex Dowdells is getting to grips with the latest technology in the treatment room.

finished I showed it to Bert, who looked at it and said, 'Yeah, excellent Davie, but put in the last paragraph, "Now I can control it, make sure I pass it to somebody in my own team."' I always thought he was a professor of the game rather than just a coach or trainer. And he was a nice man.

There were some real characters among the back-room staff to support them. Arthur Chandler was the club's record goalscorer from the 1920s and 30s, the kit man and boot man, a funny old guy. He always questioned how we could play in slippers compared to the boots that went above his ankles he was used to. David Jones was a good, strict trainer.

Alex Dowdells was a superb man at his job. He had previously been trainer with Celtic and the Scotland international side, so he had a soft spot for us Scots and we could get away with murder. We were on tour abroad during my early days at Leicester. After one of the games we had a couple of drinks with the opposition before Matt wanted us back on the team bus. When Alex was sent to collect us we were in the middle of a singsong. 'Come on you lot, it's time to get on the bus.' Frank McLintock responded by singing, 'It's a nice wee inn, the Inveraray Inn' and Alex started singing the next verse! Half an hour later Matt stormed in and shouted at Alex to get us together. Alex couldn't help himself.

George Dewis was another centre forward with the club during the 1930s and 40s. He found his niche coaching the kids and one night at Filbert Street, while having extra treatment for an injury, he called out to me, 'Davie when you have a minute, have a look at this young boy.' I wandered through to the gym, which was a concrete area of about 40 by 20 feet. This kid had laid hessian sacks on the floor and a cushion he dived on to protect his knees and elbows. Other kids were shooting at him and this youngster was throwing himself all over the gym. 'What do you think?' asked George, 'this young lad's about fourteen years old.' 'Very impressive George,' I replied. The only flaw to me was he wasn't very tall. He never grew into a giant in size but he definitely became a giant in ability, one of the finest goalkeepers England ever produced. He was of course Peter Shilton, one of the best youngsters I ever saw.

I wasn't too surprised when Gordon Banks was allowed to leave in 1967, because young Peter was a bit special. It was a tough call and possibly a slightly premature decision, but sometimes you have to give a young player his chance. I was fortunate to play with two of the greatest goalkeepers England has ever produced. I've been asked many times who was the better keeper and each time find it impossible to separate them. Perhaps Banksie's distribution when he threw the ball was slightly better. Having said that, when he threw it to me in the Cup final, I 'ballsed' it up and we lost a goal!

12

Off to the Villa

Despite its rich tradition, Aston Villa were in pretty dire straits at the end of the 1969/70 season. They tumbled into the Third Division for the first time in the club's history and manager Vic Crowe was looking to strengthen the side in an effort to bounce back quickly. The day after Leicester made me available, Vic offered me a contract. Approaching the veteran stage, he clearly felt I could help some of the youngsters.

My debut was at Wrexham in September 1970 when Willie Anderson, our winger, was injured. I was thirty-one at the time and proved I could still get into the box by scoring the first goal. I also remember crossing the ball for my old Leicester team-mate Andy Lochhead, a powerhouse of a striker, to put one away in a 3-2 win.

I didn't have to adapt my style of play in a lower division – I relied on my experience and was still fit. Perhaps I had to run a bit more as there was a little less time on the ball. If the quality pass wasn't there, you would receive the ball a second later and the space has been closed down a bit. I was realistic enough to appreciate I was just one of the squad players but enjoyed a fabulous two seasons, the highlight defeating Manchester United in the semi-final of the League Cup. I played in the third round, which we won against Northampton Town after a replay, then both legs in December 1970 against United. The first was a 1-1 draw at Old Trafford with Andy Lochhead scoring.

The return tie saw another headed goal from Andy and Pat McMahon notched the winner in front of nearly 59,000 against a very experienced side including Bobby Charlton, George Best, Paddy Crerand, Denis Law and Brian Kidd. As we came off the pitch I said to Paddy, 'I've been waiting nine years for this!' Needless to say, not only was it a marvellous result for a Third Division side, but sweet revenge for defeat in the 1963 Cup final.

Aston Villa: Dunn, Bradley, Tiler, Aitken, Turnbull, McMahon, Hamilton, Lochhead, Anderson, Gibson, Godfrey.

Manchester United: Rimmer, Sadler, Dunne, Crerand, Ure, Charlton, Morgan, Fitzpatrick, Best, Kidd, Law.

In Aston Villa's colours,
October 1970.

As mentioned earlier, I didn't have any time either for Leeds' aggressive style of play or Don Revie, even if he did play for Leicester in the 1940s. After he watched the semi, however, he did pay me a huge compliment in a newspaper article:

> In both games the star was unquestionably key midfield player Davie Gibson, who I regard as one of the most gifted individuals to emerge in Britain since the end of the War. That's no exaggeration. When Leeds were struggling in Division Two in the early 1960s, Gibson was the man I believed could put the club back on its feet. After watching him in an Army match at Catterick I was convinced he fitted the bill and received permission from the Leeds board to sign him. Unfortunately I was forced to change my mind upon learning that he had two more years of his National Service to run in Aden. Instead I signed Bobby Collins from Everton soon afterwards. Gibson has always had the ability to slow down the pace of the game when his colleagues are in difficulties, to keep the opposing defence at full stretch with tantalising long balls through the middle or down the flanks. These attributes were particularly evident against Manchester United.

The team picked itself for the League Cup final in February 1971 against Spurs other than one position, inside left. Vic Crowe had to decide whether to play me or up-and-

I'm looking at the Wembley pitch prior to the League Cup final, wondering if I might get a chance to come on during the game.

coming star Bruce Rioch, fit again after a cartilage operation. In the end the manager went for Bruce. I probably would have picked him myself, as Bruce was a goalscorer and potential matchwinner. I was sub so still felt part of the team. We put on a brave display, finally losing 2-0 to a very experienced Tottenham team including Martin Peters, Alan Mullery, Alan Gilzean and Steve Perryman, with both goals coming from that super goalscorer Martin Chivers. I don't recall too much else, I think most players have a better memory of matches won, but remember Max Bygraves entertained us at the post-match banquet as we tucked into 'Filet de Willie Anderson', 'Supreme de Volaille Rioch', 'Bombe Scare Crowe' and 'Café Curtis'. After the dinner Andy Lochhead and I, together with our wives, somehow ended up with the Spurs players at a disco on the top floor of their hotel.

Aston Villa: Dunn, Bradley, Aitken, Godfrey, Turnbull, Tiler, McMahon, Rioch, Lochhead, Hamilton, Anderson. Sub: Gibson.

Tottenham Hotspur: Jennings, Kinnear, Knowles, Mullery, Collins, Beal, Gilzean, Perryman, Chivers, Peters, Neighbour. Sub: Pearce.

Two youngsters caught my eye at pre-season training prior to the start of the 1971/72 campaign. Our coach, Ron Wylie, lined the first team up for a 3 *v.* 3 exercise in small

Aston Villa League Cup final squad, 1971. Back row: Keith Bradley, Ian Hamilton, Charlie Aitken, Pat McMahon, George Curtis, Lew Chatterley. Middle row: Ron Wylie (coach), Bruce Rioch, Andy Lochhead, John Dunn, Fred Turnbull, Michael Wright, Vic Crowe (manager). Front row: Jimmy Brown, myself, Brian Godfrey, Brian Tiler, Willie Anderson.

grids. 'Davie, your first pick.' 'I'll take that young lad with the long hair.' All the other players had their pick then it was my turn again. 'I'll take that other kid with the long hair.' They were two seventeen-year-olds and we were undefeated in the grids. Over the next few years they turned out to be two terrific professional footballers, Brian Little and John Gidman. Brian made just one appearance for England as substitute and to this day I believe he should have won more caps. The only reason in my opinion, daft as it may sound, was that he looked too scruffy. With his jersey outside his shorts and long hair, he didn't look the part playing for his country. What was that old saying, don't judge a book by its cover?

Master Gidman was the rabble rouser, a Liverpudlian apprentice. Can you believe the great Bill Shankly let him go, for failing to conform to the methods of the coaching staff at Liverpool. Like his mate at Villa, he also had long hair and didn't look like a footballer. Having a different appearance never helped young lads trying to make their way in the game, but he also annoyed one or two people along the way. While a manager's nightmare, he made it to the top at Villa, Everton and Manchester United, although to the end he gave all in authority, particularly managers, a torrid time. I still look back on my time at Villa and remember the day I picked those two young kids, who fulfilled the promise I saw in them at the training ground.

Vic Crowe was excellent, as were the coaches: Leo Crowther looked after the reserves and Ron Wylie the first team. Ron was another tough, aggressive Scot who began his career playing with the legendary Tommy Lawton at Notts County. Ron kicked the crap out of me when playing for Birmingham and there was no preferential treatment from him for me at Villa. He wasn't easily satisfied as a coach, and came up with an unusual exercise to sharpen the reflexes. He divided the first-team squad into two teams of ten. We all sat opposite each other – my number four adversary was George Curtis, a brute of a centre-half. Ron stood in the middle, bounced the ball and shouted the number. The two players would get to their feet as quickly as possible and head the ball to Ron. George and I stood up and George knocked me flying yards away before I could get anywhere near the ball. All the lads thought it was highly amusing until they discovered George had fractured my ribs and I was out of action for about six weeks.

I played four games in the 1971/72 season, the last in November 1971, a 1-0 defeat at Southend in the FA Cup. Other than missing out on the Cup final, I enjoyed every minute of my time at Villa Park in front of a wonderful partisan crowd. I only played twenty-four games for the Villa in the two years I was there, but like to think I had some small part in helping them back into the Second Division as champions at the end of the 1971/72 season.

There were some terrific guys at Villa and I roomed with right-back Keith Bradley, a good servant, pretty quick and a good tackler. Charlie Aitken at left-back was 'Mr Dependable', a Villa legend with a record number of appearances. Not many guys gave Charlie a roasting, as he was too quick for them. Brian Tiler was not a big guy at the back, but an exceptional tackler and great competitor. Fred Turnbull was a tall, lean player, reliable, very good on the ball and in the air. He was very quiet for a defender, most unusual. Brian Godfrey, 'Captain Marvel', was one of my favourites, another great competitor and winner. He was brilliant at training, never mind playing. Chico Hamilton, an elusive dribbler who could score goals. A great character in the dressing room, as he made us laugh. Pat McMahon, thin as a match but with a good engine, could run all day and ghosted into the box like Martin Peters. Willie Anderson was a great dribbler with two great feet, who could take people on.

After all these years I am still invited by Bruce Rioch's brother Neil to dinners and golf invitations with the ex-players' association, which I very much appreciate.

13

West Country Finale

My last professional club was Exeter City of the Fourth Division, where in January 1972 I once again met up with a super bunch of lads and a smashing manager in John Newman. It's never easy reaching the veteran stages of your career when a manager still has the confidence to sign you, and I was under pressure to back John's judgement. My first match was a 3-1 home defeat to Northampton and I was substituted, so not the most auspicious of starts.

Exeter: Wilson, Blain, Giles, Morris, Balson, Parker, Rowan, Morrin, Binney, Wingate, Gibson. Sub: Banks.

I would like to think that once I settled in I didn't let John down. It's not easy to please every player on your staff, but I'm certain few had cause to complain about John, who was a very dedicated professional.

I was still living in Leicester, waiting to move to our new house in Exeter, when we played at Scunthorpe. The furniture and carpet were in storage so on our way back, as we were passing through Leicester, I asked John if we could make a detour to the removal company and pick up the carpet. It was carried onto the bus by three or four of the lads and laid along the passageway. When we arrived at Exeter, the guys took it off the bus and carried it to the manager's office where it remained until Bill Diamond, an old friend, picked it up on the Monday morning, brought it to our house and had it laid before the furniture arrived a few days later. Who said footballers' lives were glamorous in those days?

We had a good year in 1972/73, finishing eighth. We stood a decent chance of promotion before we played in a snowstorm at home to Peterborough in February 1973. Tony Scott was out on the wing – he was previously at West Ham and Torquay. He was the only guy who could run down the left wing and cross the ball with his right foot, probably the best crosser of a ball I've ever seen. He must have got hundreds of crosses in – we bombarded them and got our noses in front. Then just before half-time the Peterborough left-back thundered one from 35 yards into the top corner to equalise. We've all played in games like that, when you could dominate the proceedings but the winning goal proves elusive. The next match was Southport, again at home. They were in the top two and their captain

Exeter City, 1972/73. Back row: Bob Wilson, Graham Parker, Dick Plumb, Mike Balson, Jimmy Blain, Steve Stacey, John Neale, John Wingate, Jimmy Giles, Allen Clarke. Front row: Alan Banks, Keith Clapham, Fred Binney, Tony Morrin, Tony Scott, myself, Campbell Crawford.

was John McPhee, who I remembered from Scotland. We were again the better team on the day but lost 1-0. We won only two of our remaining games and meandered out of the top four. Our form didn't desert us as we were playing well, but we were fated not to go up. I felt very sorry for John Newman but it didn't happen.

That was my first full season and I played another year, when we ended a respectable tenth in the League. One match I remember was at top-of-the-table Colchester in September 1973, when I was injured and sat on the bench next to John Newman in the dugout. It was a tight game, with no quarter given, and Graham Parker went into a crunching tackle with their centre half Stuart Morgan on the half-way line. Graham was a wee, hard, uncompromising midfielder and for once a little one beat a big 'un, as Morgan went down pole-axed. Jim Smith, the Colchester manager, jumped out of the dug-out screaming for justice at the referee with my pal and coach Bobby Roberts. With just a minute to go Colchester won a free-kick just outside the box. Unfortunately after a scramble the ball finished in the back of the Exeter net for the only goal of the match, but winning was not enough for Jim. On the final whistle the emotion of that earlier clash transformed Jim from Jekyll to Hyde, just like Frank O'Farrell earlier, as he screamed obscenities at John. John, who was shocked at the reaction, turned to me and said, 'David, get the gear.' John turned and went for Jim along the tunnel. Just as he reached the sanctuary of the dressing room, Jim turned round and saw John careering after him, with Bobby and I following him in his wake. Jim managed to lock the door, but a few seconds later John put his foot on the door and blasted it open. He grabbed Jim but before he could inflict any serious action, Bobby jumped on him and implored, 'John, don't hit him.' When tempers calmed down Bobby had saved Jim from a bloody nose. As Richard Littlejohn would say, 'You couldn't make it up!'

I also recall a hammering at Reading in February 1974 when Robin Friday, in his third League game, won the game on his own with two stunning goals in a 4-1 defeat. He was a big, strapping guy, a bit special, but sadly went off the rails.

We had a good run in the League Cup, beating West Brom 3-1 away in the third round in October 1973 when I was injured and sat with John Barnwell, who was scouting. Everyone was watching Fred Binney, a remarkable goalscorer and a good pro. He reminded me of Joe Baker – he could sniff a goal. I told John he was the best trainer in the club and you only had to look at his goalscoring record. The single piece of advice I gave Fred was that one day he'd come up against a centre half and would have to 'make' a goal. He was a bit special and, although he subsequently did well at Brighton, I could never fathom why he didn't get the opportunity to play at a higher level. We were finally beaten 5-1 in November 1973 by an experienced Wolves team that included John Richards and Dave Wagstaffe.

I had an Achilles tendon operation and was out for a couple of months during that 1973/1974 season. At the end of the year I went in to see John as I felt it was time to pack it in. I was enjoying training more than playing and didn't want to be an embarrassment. At the end of April 1974, the final match of the season at home to Rotherham was my swansong. In front of 2,945 spectators it ended goalless and the boots were hung up for the very last time.

Exeter: Wilson, Crawford, Joy, Blain, Giles, Hatch, Wallace, Binney, Bowker, Gibson, Wingate. Sub: Neale.

I did enjoy my time with the Grecians and even managed to score 3 goals in 71 appearances. As mentioned, the players were a great crowd. Alan Banks, who was one time at Liverpool, was one of the best strikers Exeter ever had. Like all goalscorers, he could sniff a chance out of the air.

Throughout my career I played with a tough wing half behind me. In Juvenile football Peter Smith was behind me. If someone kicked me Peter would say let him run through and Peter would 'have' him. As previously mentioned, Hugh Higgins at Hibs was exactly the same, as of course was Frank McLintock. However, when I ended up at Exeter and this wing half was giving me a bit of stick in one of my early games, I had to say to Jimmy Giles, our centre half, 'Jimmy, when you come up for a corner, tell the guy who's marking me if he kicks me again you'll have him.' It was only at that stage of my career did I have to ask someone to sort it out. Jimmy kicked the ball for miles and miles – his passes came to the forwards like missiles. He was a great competitor, enthusiastic and loved his football. On top of that he had the heartiest laugh you ever heard, a must in any dressing room.

Finally could I ever forget Tony Morrin or 'Chunky' as all the lads called him? What he lacked in pace, he made up with a football brain and a great touch. I wrote this poem for his fiftieth birthday, which tells you what I thought of him as a player:

Tony Morrin, a lovely fella at Exeter City.

Five o, fifty can it be true, not someone as young as you?
From Burnley town to Exeter City, if you missed him play that was a pity.
A tubby forward called Tony Morrin, was bought in those days for a florin.
Kicking and tackling wasn't his style, he never headed the ba a mile.
Thinking and passing the ba around, yes he was worth watching for a pound.
The football's over, we've gone our ways, will we ever forget those magic days?

14

Scotland Debut with a Difference

There will always be a keen debate as to when the rivalry between Scotland and England began. Was it in 1296, when old Braveheart himself defeated England at the Battle of Stirling Bridge? Or maybe 1928, when we defeated England 5-1 with the side forever known as the 'Wembley Wizards'? Or perhaps 1961, when the best England team I can recall defeated Scotland 9-3? Be it Hampden, Wembley, Twickenham or Murrayfield, for as long as Scotland play England there will always be intense rivalry.

Naturally it had always been my dream to represent Scotland but it was a difficult side to break into for valid reasons. We secured the Home Internationals in the 1961/62 season and, leading up to the England match at Wembley in April 1963, had won five Home Internationals on the spin. Leicester had been the form team in the First Division until slipping up at the end of the 1962/63 season and I was playing well, so thought I might be in the frame. The press had been very complimentary to me, especially after I had a decent game in the 2-0 win at Nottingham Forest in February 1963:

> They call him Twinkle Toes in Leicester. City fans can't remember anything like the needle-sharp ball trickster happened to them before. Forest are managed by former Scotland team manager Andy Beattie. Next day he wrote a letter to S.F.A. secretary Willie Allan on these lines – 'I have now seen Gibson three times this season and there is no better inside forward in England. The improvement in him since he came south is incredible. Not even John White of Spurs can feel safe for a national honour with Gibson around. I am convinced that if he'd been born in the south he would already be in the pool of England international players.'

In the event John White kept his place and two goals from my Army pal Jim Baxter secured a 2-1 victory against the Auld Enemy to claim the Championships again.

We'd assembled one of the strongest international squads in Europe but luck was on my side when John White was injured. We were staying away for a few days in Brighton at the beginning of May prior to the Cup final when Matt Gillies called me over. 'David congratulations, you have been called up to play for Scotland against Austria. You are to report to Glasgow and meet up with the team at Love Street, home of St Mirren for training.' It took a few minutes to take in what the manager had just said. Capped for my country, I must be dreaming.

I took the 7 p.m. train to London, then the 9.35 sleeper from St Pancras to Scotland via Leicester, as I needed a pair of boots and some extra clothes from my digs. Mike Balmer, one of our young players, packed a case for me, collected my boots at the ground and was at the station when the train pulled in. On arriving at Love Street I met up with Jim Baxter, Dave Mackay, Denis Law and Wee Willie Henderson of Glasgow Rangers. It was simply mindblowing, as it must have been for Davie Holt and Jimmy Millar, who were also making their débuts. There were two dozen telegrams from friends all over the country wishing me every success. One in particular from the secretary of my old Juvenile club, Livingston United, was special to me. It simply said, 'Your old club's best wishes tonight. J. Purdie.'

Walking out at Hampden on a beautiful evening to a crowd of over 90,000 supporters on 8 May 1963, with the pipe band playing 'Scotland the Brave' was the best moment in my career thus far. I soon worked out that 60,000 of them had to be Rangers supporters, with their favourite playing on the right wing. Every time I received the ball I gave it to Willie. The Rangers fans thought I was the 'bee's knees', I couldn't go wrong. Willie was an old-fashioned winger who, once he had the ball in his possession, never gave it back. His first thought was always, where's the full-back? There was no turning back with Willie – that was never his style.

The game began to simmer after Davie Wilson opened the scoring for us on fifteen minutes, as the Austrians thought he was offside. A linesman did have his flag up, but the goal stood and the disgruntled visitors remained in that frame of mind for the rest of the match. Ten minutes later Davie scored a second and this time the Austrian protests culminated in their huge centre forward Horst Nemec spitting at referee Jim Finney, who promptly sent him off. On twenty-eight minutes I managed to slot a pass

The telegram I received from Livingston on my Scotland debut in April 1963.

through to Denis Law, who scored the third. Soon after the break Fritz Rafreider was carried off injured on a stretcher. With an agreement to substitute outfield players until half-time only, this left Austria down to nine very unhappy men. We went 4-1 up with another goal from Law, who latched on to a defence-splitting pass by Jimmy Millar. By this time the Austrian tempers were getting very heated and they completely lost the plot. With tackles now very nasty, Erich Hof also took an early bath with a diabolical lunge at waist height on Willie Henderson. Jim decided to abandon the match with eleven minutes left after a clash between Anton Linhart and Denis Law, who the Austrians had been trying to get sent off. Jim said at the time, 'I felt I had to abandon the match or somebody would have been seriously hurt.' He was 100 per cent correct and I admired him for that.

Ian Ure told me that Nemec was the biggest centre-forward he ever played against, an absolute monster. He couldn't get off the ground he was so heavy and his nickname was 'Riesenbaby', which translates as giant baby, quite apt given his behaviour on the night. After the match there was a dinner scheduled at St Enoch Hotel in the city. Given the circumstances it seems extraordinary that it went ahead, but the two Football Associations apologised to each other and quickly sorted out any enmity. The Austrians willingly joined us and Willie Henderson even swapped his jersey with one of their players. The menu was poached salmon followed by fillet of beef, and on conclusion of the evening, with no hint of irony, there was a hearty rendition of 'Auld Lang Syne!'

We couldn't escape quickly enough from these dinners and venture out ourselves for a few drinks. We didn't speak much to the opposition after international games anyway, primarily because of the language barrier. I can't believe we had much to say to them after this match. It was a big step up to international football, but I felt confident enough to take it. That night was one of the highlights of my football career, but was also the first British international to be abandoned – what a debut!

Scotland: Brown, Hamilton, Holt, Mackay, Ure, Baxter, Henderson, Gibson, Millar, Law, Wilson.

Austria: Fraydl, Kolarik, Hasenkopf, Gager, Glechner, Koller, Linhart, Hof, Nemec, Fiala, Rafreider.

From Hampden Park we moved on to a short summer tour, playing three friendly internationals starting on 4 June at the Brann Stadian, Bergen. Not outplayed but definitely outscored by the Norwegian team, this was a game where Denis Law was in blazing form in a 4-3 defeat. Skipper Dave Mackay had been struggling with a pelvic injury and manager Ian McColl had agreed beforehand that if it flared up during the match, he was to come off. We went 2-0 up, both goals coming from Denis, but perhaps relaxed a little and let them into the game as they scored twice. We stepped up the pace and went 3-2 up in the 76th minute when Denis completed his hat-trick. When Dave Mackay signalled to the bench he was struggling, my pal Frank McLintock came on to win his first cap. Again we lowered our guard and somehow they managed to win the game with two late goals. Jim Baxter, who was not a good loser, was very unhappy – more about that later.

The Scotland side that played Austria on my debut at Hampden Park. Back row: Alex Hamilton, David Holt, Dave Mackay, Bill Brown, Ian Ure, Jim Baxter. Front row: Willie Henderson, myself, Jimmy Millar, Denis Law, Davie Wilson.

The second friendly was on 9 June at Dublin against the Republic of Ireland, another defeat, this time 1-0 courtesy of an early Noel Cantwell goal. All in all it was an excellent Irish team, including Tony Dunne, Johnny Giles and Charlie Hurley, which always raised its game when playing at Dalymount Park.

Back at the hotel after the defeat I wrote some postcards at the dinner table to send home. Although we had lost the first two games I was having a wonderful time, travelling and playing with all these superstars. So on my cards I had written 'Loving every minute, with plenty of laughs along the way.' Unfortunately Dave Mackay picked up the cards and started to read them out to Denis Law. 'Denis, are you enjoying this tour? It's the worst trip I've ever been on.' The rest of the lads joined in and gave me some fearful stick – 'Played two, lost two and you think its laughs all the way?' Talk about embarrassment. Every time we subsequently played Spurs, Dave would always greet me with – 'How's it going, laughs?' When I look back it still brings a smile to my face.

Finally on 13 June at the Bernabeu Stadium, Madrid, we faced the daunting prospect of Spain, on paper without doubt the most difficult opposition of the tour. After the two defeats, there was little confidence we could win let alone avoid a rout, especially with skipper Dave Mackay still injured. It was the end of a long, tough season, especially with the disappointment of the Cup final defeat for me, and we couldn't wait for the summer break.

Yet typically, at last the Scottish team came alive, securing a famous 6-2 victory in front of 40,000 incredulous spectators. It was a remarkable game, one where all our forwards scored: Willie Henderson, Ian St John, Denis Law, Davie Wilson and yours truly with a 20-yard daisy-cutter. My old sidekick Frank McLintock put away the third goal and we just got stuck into Spain, set about disrupting their passing game and they had no answer. Inspired as per usual by Denis Law and supported by a superb goalkeeping performance from Adam Blacklaw, we played some lovely direct football that exposed their weaknesses at the back. I guess it was a reflection of our individual talent, even if we couldn't always produce it as a team.

Ian McColl commented, 'This is one of the greatest teams ever to wear the Scottish jersey. They were all magnificent – no, superb. On this form we would have beaten the best side in the world.' A year later Spain won the European Championships on their own soil, with captain Feliciano Rivilla, the Real Madrid star Amaro and Carlos Lapetra survivors from this rout. It remains Spain's heaviest-ever home defeat.

Scotland: Blacklaw, McNeill, Holt, McLintock, Ure, Baxter, Henderson, Gibson, St John, Law, Wilson.

Spain: Vicente Train, Rivilla, Mingorance, Reija, Aguirre, Glaría, Amaro, Rodriguez, Veloso, Guillot, Lapetra.

Cap number five arrived in October 1963 against Northern Ireland at Windsor Park, Belfast in the Home Internationals. We suffered a 2-1 defeat, Ian St John scoring our goal. Ireland had a decent side featuring Harry Gregg, Terry Neill, Billy Bingham and Johnny Crossan. For the next four internationals I was excluded from the squad. Was it the laughs, was it the Ireland defeat, surely it wasn't my ability, was my international career over?

I returned for the Wales game at Ninian Park on 3 October 1964 and even managed a goal in the first half. After a neat move involving Jimmy Johnstone and Denis Law, Stevie Chalmers flicked it through to me in the box and in turn I glanced it past Gary Sprake. We were 2-1 up with about four minutes to play and Jim Baxter and Denis Law had been 'showboating'. They thought the game was won, when Ken Leek popped up to score twice in the last two minutes. It was a sad end to a match I was enjoying, having scored and made the other for Stevie Chalmers, who was making his international debut. I should have realised that over the years with Scotland certain triumph is only one violent lurch away from impending disaster. One of the highlights was playing against Ivor Allchurch, one of Wales' finest footballers, and playing with a young man who became one of the greatest dribblers Scotland or any other country has ever seen. It was Jimmy Johnstone's first international and he was ultimately awarded by their supporters the honour of the greatest Celtic player of all time.

Our World Cup campaign commenced on 21 October 1964 against Finland at Hampden. A satisfying 3-1 win at last with goals from Denis Law (two minutes), a header from Stevie Chalmers (thirty-eight minutes) and the third myself after forty-two minutes when I guided the ball into the net from 20-yards. I felt that I linked up well with Alex Scott on the night, but sadly that was the end of my Scotland career. I remained in the squad but was never picked again.

A precious international goal against Wales at Ninian Park in October 1964. Gary Sprake is the keeper left on the ground.

Six international games on and the wheels fell off when we lost 2-1 to Poland at Hampden, missing out on World Cup qualification for the 1966 tournament in England. Years later I met up with Willie Henderson. The Spanish game was mentioned, as were many more, until I brought up the Poland fixture. I said to Willie that I thought our manager Jock Stein had made a mistake in his selection. 'What do you mean?' asked Willie. 'Well he picked Billy Bremner to play alongside you instead of me.' Willie replied, 'But wee Billy was very good.' 'I agree, but Billy was a tackler, whereas I was a passer of the ball. I would have given you many more passes than Billy.' 'Aye I see what you mean,' said Willie. I mentioned that with absolutely no disrespect to Billy. It was his second cap, he was the man in form and it would have been a tough call to leave him out.

The memories of playing with some outstanding footballers for Scotland more than made up for that disappointment. I was capped seven times for my country, scoring three wonderful goals – well I thought they were. Although of course I would love to have played more, I couldn't complain. Perhaps it had something to do with playing for a less fashionable club, or represented an era when the majority of players selected were still playing in the Scottish League, probably for Rangers or Celtic. After all, Frank McLintock only managed nine caps and he was a great player.

The Scotland team for the Wales game. Back row: Alex Hamilton, Jim Kennedy, John Greig, Ron Yeats, Jim Baxter, Campbell Forsyth. Front row: Jimmy Johnstone, Stevie Chalmers, Denis Law, myself, Jimmy Robertson.

Competing with Denis Law, Billy Bremner, the elusive Charlie Cooke and John White for the two inside forward positions, it was always going to be tough. The White family featured prominently during my life. There were three brothers: John, Tom, who was demobbed on the same day as me, and Edwin, who played for Falkirk at the same time as John. Tom and Edwin were like bookends, big and strong battlers, while John was like me in stature and of course Matt Gillies tried unsuccessfully to sign him before he went to Spurs. John's withdrawal through injury enabled me to make my debut against Austria and poignantly, subsequent to his tragic death by lightning at the tender age of twenty-seven in July 1964, I regained my place against Wales.

A few months after John died I was selected to play for a Scotland XI in his testimonial match organised at White Hart Lane against Spurs. On the evening the game was due to be played, it was very foggy and couldn't go ahead. It was quickly rescheduled for the following day (11 November 1964), but unfortunately Leicester had a League Cup tie against Crystal Palace so I couldn't make it. Guesting for Spurs was John's brother Tom, who scored one of the goals when Jimmy Greaves slipped him in. All the Scotland players were presented with an inscribed canteen of cutlery, even though in the event I didn't actually play. I played just once for the international side alongside John in the Northern Ireland game, but was pitted against him many times in the First Division. He was like a gazelle, a quiet, lovely lad and another I felt privileged to come across on my journey.

Even the most determined optimist would concede that watching the game is nothing like playing. However, it's the next best thing and, my Scotland career over, my pal Jack McLay and I bought two tickets on the terracing for the friendly against Brazil in June 1966 at Hampden Park. It was part of the build-up to the World Cup finals (for Brazil) and we were looking forward to seeing Pele in the flesh, but unfortunately Billy Bremner and John Clark had other ideas in a 1-1 draw.

During the second half a young Scottish supporter stood next to us, swaying backwards and forwards as drunks do, shirt unbuttoned and pissed out of his mind. Instead of watching the game he was facing up the terracing and I said to him, 'Don't you want to see Pele play?' He paused for a moment then slurred a memorable one-liner, 'For all I know it could be f***g Louis Armstrong!' Where do they find these gems?

In 1977 I travelled from the West Country to London to meet some old pals who were down for the Scotland *v*. England match. We met at a modest guesthouse and in the evening went out on the town for a few bevvies, getting warmed up for the following day. When I came down for breakfast on the Saturday morning, a few of the guys still hadn't sobered up and one of them broke into a song. Someone shouted across the room, 'Davie, it's not very often you get a cabaret with your breakfast.' At around midday the taxis arrived to take us to the ground, but unfortunately we were one cab short, so four of us had to make our way to Wembley on the underground. When the train doors opened I couldn't believe my ears – I thought everyone who had travelled down from Scotland was on that tube. Most were dressed in kilts, banners wrapped around them, singing every Scottish song that has ever been written. It was standing room only and I felt like a fish out of water, dressed up, collar and tie with my overnight bag, looking everything but a Scottish supporter. As I stood facing this well-oiled fan, he looked me up and down and quickly decided I was the enemy. In true Glaswegian twang he let rip with, 'If it wasn't for you English bastards, I would have a ticket.' I didn't have the balls to explain that I was Scottish and did in fact once play for my country. Gordon McQueen scored the winning goal in a famous 2-1 victory and to top it all off the supporters in their hysteria ran onto the pitch and broke the crossbar. My mate on the underground must have got a ticket somehow as I'm sure I saw him swinging on the bar!

15

Life After Football

My career was over, the adulation dimmed, so whatever next? As a family man the common path of running a pub was out of the question and staying in football never appealed to me. I wanted to enjoy being at home and as a coach or manager I would have forever been going in the opposite direction to my family. We'd already opened a little hairdresser's salon in Stoney Stanton, where we were living. Mavis' sister was the hairdresser and we ran that for about five years. It was my first step towards becoming a millionaire, but it didn't quite happen!

Then out of the blue the opportunity to run a garden shop turned up in Exmouth, not that I knew anything about running that type of business. Fortunately two elderly gentlemen well into their sixties called Cliff and Cyril came with the shop. Over the following five years plants, dog food and invoices became the order of the day. Cliff worked out the price of materials and calculated the markup in his head, jotting it all down in pencil. One day I offered him a modern machine called a calculator. He trusted his mind and pencil but eventually had a go at modern technology.

During my football career I met some fascinating people, but meeting Bill Harris was up there with the best of them. A phone call to the shop was my first introduction to Bill. He was a retired gardener ordering some plants and soil, which I delivered in the van at the end of the day. This white-haired old man was sitting in the kitchen and his first words were, 'Cup of tea, son?' followed by, 'Fill the kettle, get the cake out of the cupboard.' I must have heard those words a thousand more times as he entertained me with stories of his life as a professional gardener. From then on, every weekend my kids and I would drive 300 yards to Bill's house to deliver the Sunday lunch my wife had prepared and we never left empty-handed. Bill put potatoes, carrots, peas, cauliflower and lettuce into bags for Mavis and over the next five years I learnt his life story.

He started his business in Budleigh Salterton, close to the golf course. He would venture out very early in the morning on to the eighteenth green, shoot the rabbits and sell them to the local butcher. He made enough money to build his own greenhouse, which he named appropriately 'Rabbits'. When one of the local members of the W.I. complained about his plants, he gave the lady a new box on the condition that she never returned to his garden centre. Wise man, Bill – the lady told everyone at the

W.I. she had been banned, so they all knew Bill had a garden centre. When another lady complained about the condition of her geranium in a 5-inch pot, Bill put it back with new soil in a 7-inch pot. 'That's much better,' she said. At eighty-two Bill had two replacement hips and retired to live with his son in Falmouth. I kept in touch with him and he made it to a century, a very special friend.

After five years in the shop it was time for a change – back to our English roots in Leicestershire. I became a postman in Earl Shilton, walking the streets, cycling or driving the van to farms in the area. I enjoyed the life, out in all weathers, meeting new people, and it gave me peace of mind. I was only back a few days when Alan Birchenall gave me a ring – 'Gibbo we need you to play for the Old Stars Charity team.' Geriatrics would be nearer the truth. Playing for the Leicester Old Stars brought the fun back again – if you lost the ball nobody gave you a bollocking for not getting back to defend. You were too busy getting your breath back after doing your best to get up the other end. For the next four years it was really enjoyable although the following day you paid for it. All went well until a fateful day at Corby Town, when I pulled my boots on for the very last time. I knew the end had come when I lasted just four minutes and the old hamstring went again. It was with great sadness that I had to tell Birch I was retiring from the team as my little legs had run out of gas.

After retiring as a postie I wondered what to do next. I had a chance to take a pub but then an offer arose out of the blue to take over an old peoples' home in Leicester. I

The postman calls. Cycling my round at Earl Shilton beats walking the street for a living.

met a mosaic tiler from Sardinia called Fizz Phuddi who left his *nom de plume* all over town. When he realised who I was he took a shine to me and, as he was already in the business, said he had an empty house for sale in Whetstone with planning permission to convert into an old peoples' home. I spoke to different friends but couldn't raise the finance, then one of the lads I knew from Villa suggested a finance company. Just as I was about to sign the agreement I played a round of golf at Cosby Golf Club with a bank manager, who warned me they were moneylenders that charged exorbitant interest. He managed to arrange the finance for me so I was very fortunate to escape. We had our own separate living quarters and it was perfect for the kids and us. We also built a flat above the garage and housed fourteen bedrooms in the end. It was homely and became one of the best care homes in the area. We were on duty in the flat in case any of the alarms went off, etc. One night the bell went and I looked through the window to be greeted by Social Services. They were checking up on us as we had also bought a bungalow over the road and they wanted to make sure we were still living in the peoples' home. The lady from Social Services didn't realise it was me at the window – she thought I was one of the residents!

We had fourteen staff, Mavis was the manager/matron and I was the maintenance man (and entertainer). It was a very satisfying time but had its moments. The fire officer came in one year and insisted I knock a gate through a back wall into the alleyway as an additional means of escape. Eventually I got a local brickie to cut it out and the moment he finished, the neighbours the other side complained that it had reduced the value of their homes by £3,000. Some of them built a gate at the end of the alleyway and locked it to prevent the route from being viable. It was all very petty, I was out of pocket and in the end the alley was never used and we had to put another door through the lounge instead.

We sold up in 2002 and moved to Sturminster Newton in order to live closer to the family. I took a part-time job as a driver running a couple of disabled children to a local school for a year, then my daughter Kay asked me to clean her windows. As a direct result I built up a little window-cleaning business in the area. However, having fallen from a ladder towards the end of 2012, I now restrict myself to the ground floor and a youngster scales the heights for me!

I still find a bit of time to devote to my beloved golf and now play off a handicap of eleven at a beautiful course on the outskirts of Yeovil. My little legs have managed to get me around many a course all over the world and some years ago at Cosby a gentleman came over and introduced himself. 'See that little lad practising putting? I named him after you and he wants to be a golfer.' I replied that I hoped he would become a better golfer than I was a footballer. This little boy David Gibson turned out to be one of the best golfers Leicestershire has produced over the last forty years. He won more events than any other local golfer and made it to the finals of the *Daily Mail* Fours with his young son. In 1997 I was privileged to play with David in a Cosby competition, the Captain's Trophy. I remember standing on the first tee praying I wouldn't let young David down. It wasn't until we were walking up the thirteenth fairway that he asked me if I was enjoying myself. 'Not really, we've played twelve holes and I'm not on the card yet.' 'But you've played in front of 100,000 people at Wembley.' 'Yes,' I replied,

Cousin Tommy Sneddon and I pursuing our great passion of golf at St Andrews in 2003.

'but if my memory serves me right I didn't play too well there either.' David was three under par and I was anticipating the moment I might be required to par or birdie one of the remaining six holes. David parred the twelfth, fourteenth and fifteenth holes. He would have parred the sixteenth but for once I managed to get a putt for par before he had a put for a birdie. I'm on the card.

On the seventeenth David hit another up the middle, while yours truly was 40 yards shorter and to the right of the fairway. With a stream running in front of the green, I said I usually played a 9-iron short of the brook, chipped onto the green and hopefully putt for a four. David said, 'Play a 5-iron – take on the green but don't worry, I'll get a four anyway.' Unbelievably he landed in the brook. I took out my five iron and thinned it. How it ever got over the brook I'll never know. The ball missed the bridge by inches, hit the inside bank and came to rest on the apron, some 30 feet from the flag. My worst fears had finally arrived – two putts for par with my nerves jangling. I did manage to make a par that, with one shot off, made it a three. The final hole was another par four. Again David smacked his drive away up the middle and once more I was about forty yards short of him. David asked me what I thought. I told him I usually played an 8-iron off the green, taking the bunkers out of the equation, chipped on and took my chance with a putt. 'No,' said David, 'play a 3-iron, take on the green but don't worry, I'll get a four.' I wish I had his confidence. Out came the 3-iron, I hit it well but a shade to the right as it went sailing towards a row of trees. Now if I didn't get lucky at Wembley, Lady Luck shone on me this time as the ball clipped a twig just enough to divert it towards the green, where it finished 3 feet from the flag. I managed to putt a birdie and looked to the heavens. David actually put his second shot into the bunker and later in the clubhouse we discovered my birdie on the last won us the tournament. Over twenty years as a footballer I had some wonderful memories, but that day playing at Cosby is up there with the best of them – thanks David.

Football, golf, cricket, I've tried my hands and feet at them. I was reasonably good at football, not bad at golf but absolutely hopeless at cricket. My first introduction to cricket was soon after I signed for Hibernian, when a charity match was arranged against Leith Franklin, a local Edinburgh side. 'Can anyone play cricket?' our old trainer shouted. One or two hands were raised but we were well short of a team. He then called out the names of all the youngsters in the team. 'You lot are playing next week, be there or your football career could be over before it starts.' With no idea how to bat, I asked the trainer if I could possibly go in last. Leith Franklin scored 160 for four, then, to make a game of it, their opening bowler ran up ever so slowly, bowled a full toss and our openers put on a few runs. We were edging our way towards the Leith total when, with just ten runs needed we were down to the last man – me. Needless to say they were determined not to lose to a bunch of kids. As I stood at the wicket the umpire said to me, 'What do you want?' A gentle full toss to get me off the mark would be fine. The quick bowler on the horizon disappeared but soon came flying towards me like a young Harold Larwood. In a split second I wondered what the hell I had done to deserve this. I now knew why the first team players hadn't volunteered to play – if this missile hits me, my football career is over. Instinct told me to lift my bat – crash – the bails and stumps went flying. I turned and there was the umpire with his finger up, smiling at me – a blind man could see I was out. Smiling back, I remember saying, 'Who cares – I'm bloody well still alive.'

About six years later I played my second and final game. It was another friendly, this time at Leicester against a county eleven, and again that familiar cry went up in the dressing room, 'Can anyone play cricket?' 'Yes I can and I could possibly open the batting.' Maybe I can't bat but I have a good memory – those gentle full tosses sprang to mind. The Leicestershire side scored over 200 runs and I opened the innings full of confidence. Awaiting the arrival of my first ball I glanced at the opening bowler, a giant of a man. He was one of the fastest bowlers Australia ever produced, Graham McKenzie. He was ever so kind to me – instead of his usual 40-yard run up he slid behind the umpire and took a couple of strides. I never saw the ball until I heard that familiar sound of three flying stumps once more. My cricket career was over, but thankfully I lived to tell the tale. At the other end was a slow bowler called Tony Lock, who played a mere 49 Tests for England. I remember a shuffling as spin bowlers do, before he sent the ball down. Bobby Roberts came forward and was bowled by a bloody orange.

16

The Best Team of All, My Family

Mum and Dad were both Hearts fanatics, home and away. I was only a kid when we all went to Tynecastle for a Scottish Cup tie in front of a full house of over 30,000. Being a youngster my uncle took me down to the front, away from the masses still coming in for the game. There was no seating and you had to be in the ground an hour before the start to secure a favourite viewpoint. A few minutes before kick-off the stadium was heaving and a bit of panic was setting in with the supporters. The fans behind me started whistling and waving their handkerchiefs – that was the signal someone in the crowd was in trouble. The ambulance people arrived quickly with their stretcher and who would be walking past me but mum and my aunt Martha, Matt for short, with dad on the stretcher. They were taken to the treatment room, and then later allowed back to a safer place in the ground. Back home, dad told me that, as mum and aunt Matt were panicking in the crowd, he sized up the situation, waved his white hanky and, being on the small side of wee, was transported down the terracing. As they were standing in the tunnel, the teams were waiting to enter the field. Mum's hero, Willie Bauld, was only about 3 feet away from her, she was as close as she ever would be, so close she could have touched him. She wanted to say 'Good luck' to Willie but froze and never had another chance to speak to her hero. By the way, dad hadn't fainted, he saw mum was in trouble and reacted quickly. All mum was worried about was not speaking to her hero.

After signing for Hibernian I met one of the old men in the village, a pal of my dad, and he did bring me down to earth with the one-liner, 'Congratulations Davie, son. You might be a good footballer, but you will never be as good a man as your father.' I never forgot those words.

When I was transferred to Leicester City my wages were £17 a week. When I returned the following season (1962/63), the players were given an £8 per week rise, so I was now on the dizzy heights of £25 a week. It was around this time that Frank McLintock and Gordon Banks went into Matt Gillies' office to ask for a rise in wages. They felt they were worthy of a few more bob and were asking for an additional £10 per week. Matt had a silver tongue and was a difficult man to pin down where money was concerned. The board still held the upper hand when it came to wages, even allowing for the abolition of the maximum wage in 1961. It threatened to become nasty but they eventually got their rewards. On hearing the news Colin Appleton complained that, as captain, he had been told all the players would be on the same wage. As a result we all soon received a rise of £10, so Frank and Gordon went straight back into the manager's office to ask for another £10 a week rise. 'No luck this time,' said Matt. 'You asked for another tenner and received it, but what you really want is a tenner more than the rest and you are definitely not getting another rise.' It's still difficult to believe that international players like Frank and Gordon were treated in that way. Back at the oil works dad would probably have been earning £6-7 a week. I phoned him to mention I had just received another rise, bringing my wages up to £35 a week. I never will forget his reply: 'Who the hell needs £35 a week to live?'

In 1964 the average weekly wage was £16. I signed a new two year contract that year with my basic wages at £60, a week rising to £70 if we occupied second, third or fourth place in the League and £85 if we were top, so we didn't do too badly. It was quite a complex document, as there was also provision for an additional £250 as a current international, £300 paid bi-monthly, £5 per thousand on gates over 30,000 and bonuses in the FA Cup, from £20 for winning the third round, through to £400 if we won the Cup.

No matter how much I earned in my career, I never felt as contented as my dad. In all the years playing football my father only ever gave me one piece of advice. It was always the same, be it as a schoolboy, juvenile and even when a professional. After every game he'd say, 'You still need a yard.' I think he liked what he saw, but it was his way of keeping my feet on the ground and not getting too carried away. I'm sure he meant I was not the quickest footballer on the planet but I always told him that I was quick between my ears.

While at Leicester, mum and dad came down now and then for a holiday and to see me play, travelling mainly by bus and later by train. On one occasion I lost both of them at Birmingham railway station. Their train was due to arrive on platform nine. I waited and waited but there was no sign of them and, as they were getting on a bit I panicked, thinking they may have missed their stop. I returned to the ticket office to make sure the train had arrived; it had twenty minutes ago. Not knowing where to look, I was making my way back to the car when away along the platform I spotted dad. 'Where have you been?' I asked a little too loudly, but relieved I had found them. Little or not, dad came flying back with, 'Where the hell have you been? Your mother has been sitting here for over twenty minutes and she is frozen.' The train had arrived on a different platform, not that I was psychic.

Years later, when mum had passed away and dad was nearing ninety, he came down for another visit, this time in style. For the first time in his life he travelled by plane and I waited for him at East Midlands airport. Every passenger had come off the plane; no dad, not again, where is he this time? Surely you can't get lost on a plane. Eventually he came around the corner, followed by an air hostess carrying his case. 'Enjoy the flight dad?' I ventured. 'There's no other way to travel,' he replied. He smiled and thanked the air hostess for helping with his suitcase. At ninety he was still a better man than I ever will be. Sadly, sister Mary passed away in 1997.

Somewhere between the football matches I met my future wife, Mavis Clifford. On our first date in 1963 at the Crown pub, Gilmorton I gave her my telephone number

Mum and Dad at Winchburgh Bowling Club on the occasion of their golden wedding anniversary in 1983. Family members are: Stephen, Craig, Jack (brother-in-law) and sister Mary, myself and Mavis, Kay, Stuart and Ciona.

and she duly phoned me up. While I had the wee Ford Anglia I still had 'L'-plates, but Mavis had passed her test so drove us to another pub just outside Leicester. At the end of the evening we stopped at the bottom of the road to my digs and I said, 'If I was a nice boy I would ask you out again.' She replied, 'But you are a nice boy.' I'd cracked it. The next date was an evening out in Coventry – this time I drove. Nearing the city, the traffic lights changed too quickly in my opinion and I had to perform an emergency stop. As it was a two-door car, I braked so hard Mavis' front passenger seat shot forward and she nearly flew through the windscreen. How to make an impression.

Mavis' father Walter was a Foxes fan, so that might have worked in my favour as well. On the way home from taking Mavis to a Leicester match, she remarked how good a player Mike Stringfellow was. 'The wee Scots boy is better,' was her father's wise response.

We married in November 1966 at a registrar's office in Hinckley, as it was close to where Mavis' mother lived. There were twelve wedding guests and the best man was Stan Brown, friend of all the Leicester players for over forty years. Stan was a lovely, funny man who I think worked as a comedian on the local circuit for a time. Every Friday afternoon after training I always headed for Stan and Mary's for Scotch pie, chips and gravy – it almost became a pre-match ritual. Then we would go out with them on Saturday nights. Jon Sammels, who had a distinguished career with the Foxes and then Arsenal, was another great friend of Stan and Mary, visiting them when I left Leicester, and to this day Jon still sees Mary in an old people's home.

Our wedding day in November 1966.

Stan doubled up as our taxi driver, picking Mavis up en route to the registrar's office. The ceremony was followed by a reception meal at a restaurant, or more correctly the local pub, the Star Inn at Stoney Stanton. If my memory serves me right the bill for the whole day was less than £50! In the evening we went to see Mike and Bernie Winters at the Coventry Theatre, followed by a one-night stand at the Leofric Hotel in Coventry. So we married on the Thursday, trained back at Leicester on the Friday and we beat Burnley 5-1 on the Saturday mentioned earlier, followed by a party in the evening. The game was on *Match of the Day* with Kenneth Wolstenholme commentating and I scored a great goal. I chipped my fellow Scot Adam Blacklaw, who was an excellent keeper – I should have played against him every week. It was a wonderful three days but that brilliant chip took a lot of beating.

I'm certain every footballer that played in the 1960s will have their favourite Bill Shankly story – I was no exception. For example, during a five-a-side training session Chris Lawler was asked by Shanks whether or not he'd scored a goal or was he offside. Chris replied, 'Sorry boss, you were offside.' 'Christ son,' said Bill, 'You've been here four years, hardly said a word and when you do, you're a bloody liar!' On 6 October 1967, I was present at the birth of our son at 7.45 p.m. in Bond Street Maternity Hospital, Leicester. I'd arranged to meet a friend at the Grand Hotel to celebrate the birth. We were playing Liverpool the next day and, as I walked into the hotel, who was pacing the foyer but Shanks. 'Hello son,' were Bill's first words. 'Bill, my wife has just given birth to a little boy.' 'Call him Bruce, son, it's a good Scottish name.' We called him Stuart, sorry Bill! We beat Liverpool 2-1 the next day, all in all a wonderful weekend. Fortunately or unfortunately Stuart didn't take after me – although he was very good and enjoyed all sports, he didn't have one special passion. Instead he took after his granddad – a simple life, a pint, a fag and a sporting chronicle, and he was happy. He's also an excellent partner to have in your sports quiz team, he's always posing me an obscure question and I love him to bits.

We were also delighted when he gave us our first granddaughter, Hannah. From about the age of two I took Hannah swimming. Well, strictly speaking there was more laughing, jumping and diving into the pool than swimming. However, after about a year and many bribes of chocolate from the candy machine (my way of coaching), she would try to swim one width of the baths and finally made it.

In April 1969 we lost the Cup final, then a few weeks later were relegated. That was the saddest day of my football career, but 1969 was not all bad news. On 15 December Mavis gave birth to our elder daughter Ciona at the maternity hospital in Salisbury – now she did take after me. Well maybe I'm being a little selfish as her mum was a reasonable sports competitor at school, winning the Victrix Ladorum as her daughter did many years later.

When Ciona was about three years old we visited a Hotel in Swanage. Mave and I were sitting in the lounge while Stuart and Ciona were running around the place. The proprietor asked if we would like some drinks, which were laid on the table, and the kids joined us. Ciona was sitting next to me, her little legs dangling in front of her, when all of a sudden she put her feet up to the side of the table and pushed. To this day I can still see it in slow motion as the table tipped over and all the drinks slid down and smashed over the lounge carpet. She may have only been three years old but her brain was going at 50 mph. She jumped up and started running with her Dad in hot pursuit – I couldn't believe a three-year-old could run so fast. She was only saved when the proprietor said, 'Mr Gibson don't panic it's only a drink!' Running, hockey, netball – she took them all in her stride and after leaving school learnt to play golf. Of the few golfing trophies I won, winning the Mixed Open with Ciona at Cosby Golf Club has to be one of my proudest moments.

Inevitably a tall, handsome stranger entered the arena – Paul Nicholson, now my son-in-law. They walked up the aisle to Al Jolson's 'The Bells Are Ringing For Me and My Girl', another of my proudest moments. They have given us two grandsons, Harry and Freddie, and our granddaughter Martha.

On 6 July 1971 Kay arrived. It is true to say wherever Kay goes she brings a breath of fresh air to the proceedings, exuding enthusiasm in everything she does. A swimming gala between local schools was held at Hinckley Leisure centre and the last event of the night was the relay race. Unfortunately the Earl Shilton School was one swimmer short, therefore could not enter a team. That was until Kay proposed to her teacher, 'Sir, why can't I swim the first *and* last leg then we could at least take part?' The proposal was accepted by the other schools, but alas there was no fairy-tale ending. After all this was Kay at Hinckley Leisure Centre and not Esther Williams at Hollywood. The swimmers were all dried and changed when Kay made it to the finishing line. As they say in the movies, 'The kid's got guts' – she volunteered and came in last, but for me it is still a magical memory.

Keeping to a sporting theme, both girls enrolled for lessons at the local ballet school. Every week they went for tuition and on returning home demonstrations were performed on the lounge carpet. While Ciona could float like a butterfly Kay would

Our wonderful children: Stuart, Kay, myself, Mavis and Ciona at a wedding in 1999.

A family montage.

The Gibson grandchildren.

trip over her own shadow, but to her credit she never missed a lesson. On leaving school, Liverpool University beckoned and after three years of study, on 2 July 1993 Kay earned a Bachelor of Education. Mavis and I were proud parents at John Moores University on the day she walked forward to receive her honours degree. Kay is married to James, a super dad and terrific son-in-law, who gave Mavis and I two wonderful grandchildren, Anya and Angus.

I am indebted to Billy Gillies from Jedburgh, who was in the Army with me and wrote this poem called 'Reflections on Reaching 70' to mark my birthday.

> On getting dressed the other night, I looked in the mirror and got such a fright.
> I could not take in what I was seeing, the state of me took some believing.
> My face it has begun to line, am I getting old, is this the sign?
> The closer I went the worse it got, the mirror reflecting every spot.
> My hair it is now receding, I'm turning grey, that's all I'm needing.
> What's happened to my grand crop of hair, for all I see there's not much there.
> Shaving in the mirror every day, ne'er attention did I pay.
> Maybe I did ne'er want to see, this ageing lark creeping up on me.
> Where has it gone my youthful figure, what was there has got much bigger.
> The muscles that once stood out proud, what's happened to them for crying out loud?
> My belly it's begun to sag, my backside's drooping like a tattie bag.
> And look at those legs that once held power, alas as for me the football's o'er
> But that's not me it cannot be, is it, it is!

I find it hard to believe I'm now in my mid-seventies when I still feel about thirty – where have all the years gone? I've enjoyed most of it, particularly growing up in the miners' rows at Winchburgh. As kids we never had material things, so you didn't miss much. What we did was fun – swimming in the canal, stealing apples out of the orchard and more importantly kicking the wee tanner ba that changed my life. I have been very fortunate with my family. Over the years I have tried to make my fortune one way or another, but realise it's your children and grandchildren that are your fortune. They provide amazing returns for the whole of your life, none more so that our first grandchild. I penned this ode on Harry's birth:

> Harry, you made your entrance early, simply couldn't wait
> Little arms and tiny legs on that September date.
> You must have known the happiness the pleasure that you'd bring
> By arriving four weeks early our hearts began to sing.
> You are my first wee grandson, a treasure to be found
> All my love and attention is yours when I'm around.
> I hope to be around sometime and watch you progress
> Be sport for Wales or Scotland I won't be too distressed.
> No matter what your choice is, whatever path you take
> I'm right behind you Harry, I'll always be your mate.

17

Seven Magnificent Scots, Three Goalkeepers and an Englishman

I guess all pros believe their era was the best to play in and I'm not against the modern game at all. Personally, I believe players from the 1950s were more entertaining than any other generation. Some people might say that current footballers who are paid £100,000+ per week makes them better players, but they certainly don't seem to enjoy themselves as much as we did. I believe every generation had great players and I'd like to highlight some of my favourites.

My own hero was Heart of Midlothian legend Willie Bauld, part of the 'Terrible Trio' of Conn, Bauld and Wardhaugh. I first encountered Willie at the age of ten in October 1948 when he made his debut for Hearts. My older cousin Tommy Sneddon took me to the match, where the opponents were East Fife. It was also the first time these three young men appeared together at Tynecastle, much to the dismay of defenders throughout the country. Alfie Conn was number 8, Willie Bauld number 9 and Jimmy Wardhaugh sported 10. Hearts rattled in six that day, with Willie grabbing three and Alfie two. To prove it was no flash in the pan, the following week Willie scored another hat-trick as Queen of the South were hammered 4-0.

Over the following twelve years or so it was Willie, labelled 'King of Hearts', who became the favourite son of nearly 30,000 Hearts supporters. When the local supporters' bus travelled to the games I was right there at the front, trying to look hard over the retaining wall to see my hero. Jimmy Wardhaugh finished top scorer of the three with 206 League goals to his credit. Willie scored 183 goals from 292 League games, missing a fair number of matches because of injury. Although Alfie Conn didn't score regularly, he still packed a shooting power with his spectacular drives from a distance and found the net 115 times in 223 League matches. The threesome played their last game together in the George Dobbie testimonial match against Raith Rovers at Tynecastle in October 1960, when Wardhaugh and Conn were guests for the club that night. Willie won two League Cup winners' medals, a Scottish Cup winners' medal and two Championship medals.

Sadly, an incident on his international debut at Hampden in 1950 was to scar Willie for the rest of his life. Scotland needed a draw or win against England to reach the World Cup finals in Brazil as British champions. With England leading 1-0, Willie passed up the best chance of the match, hammering a shot against the crossbar that he would

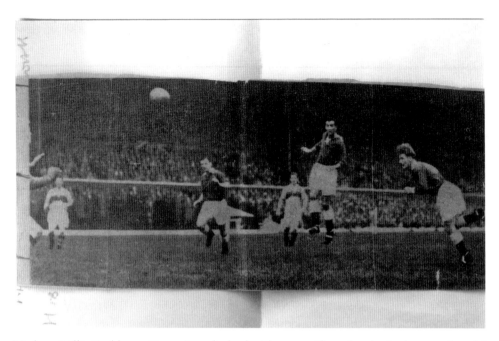

My hero Willie Bauld puts Hearts into the lead with a magnificent header in the 1954 Scottish League Cup final against Motherwell.

normally have buried. He played again against Switzerland and scored, but his third cap a month later against Portugal in Lisbon was his last, although he again found the net. Lawrie Reilly, a magnificent centre forward, took over his spot – Scotland couldn't drop Lawrie, he was that good. Willie won thirteen Scottish League caps, scoring 15 times, including 5 against the League of Ireland in 1958, but his lack of international success was simply due either to injury or the quality of players like Lawrie competing with him during those years. When he died in 1977, just nine months before Jimmy Wardhaugh at the tender age of forty-nine, the whole city of Edinburgh grieved and Gorgie Road was silenced as the funeral cortège passed by.

Willie was a deceptive player with an unhurried style that sometimes attracted criticism. In fact, his football brain was always thinking ahead and his burst of activity usually proved effective. There are thousands of people who play football, but only hundreds with football brains. They're the special footballers and Willie was one of them. An outstanding header of the ball, only 5 feet 8 inches tall, he was equally skilled with either foot and packed a clinical finish.

In the 1940s Mr W. S. Allison presented a trophy to be played annually between an Edinburgh Select XI and one of the top English sides. Over £90,000 was raised for charitable causes and in 1961 I was delighted to be picked for the team to play Burnley, one of the strongest English sides at the time. Who was the centre forward playing alongside me? Yes, Willie Bauld, fourteen years after I saw him play his first game. As fairy tales go this was among the best of them, even more so when I managed to score a hat-trick in the first half.

18,500 fans were treated to a high-scoring match, with four goals in the opening ten minutes, including my first. After twenty-five minutes I was fouled in the box and took the penalty myself. Then, to complete my hat-trick, I managed to slot the ball past Adam Blacklaw two minutes from the break. However, it was my opening goal that I'll never forget. I gathered the ball about 35 yards from the Burnley goal. Willie Bauld was standing around the semi-circle of the 18-yard line. My one thought was if I pass the ball to Willie and he lays it off, I might get a shot from just outside the penalty area. Instead of laying it back to me, Willie turned the other way and all the defenders moved across, expecting him to hit it on the turn. They forgot about me and I kept running into the penalty area when, either by pure magic or telepathy, Willie deftly cut the ball back. I was still running and scored from about 8 yards. It was the greatest goal I scored, all thanks to my hero and the only hat-trick I managed in my career.

We lost 7-4 to a brilliant Burnley performance, with two other hat-tricks courtesy of Jimmy Robson and England centre forward Ray Pointer, but it didn't detract from one of the happiest days of my career.

One local newspaper reported, 'He's got legs like a manicure tweezer but what a football brain he has. Willie Bauld grew younger every time he raced down the Easter Road field with Gibson. This was spoon feeding at speed.'

Edinburgh Select: Simpson, Fraser, Holt, Polland, Easton, Baxter, Scott, Gibson, Bauld, Docherty, Hamilton.

Burnley: Blacklaw, Angus, Elder, Joyce, Adamson, Miller, Connelly, McIlroy, Pointer, Robson, Harris.

From my hero and the 'Terrible Trio' to Lawrie Reilly and Gordon Smith, two of the 'Famous Five' – Smith, Johnstone, Turnbull, Reilly and Ormond. The north (home) stand at Easter Road is named after them and in Hibernian's rich history, no group of players has ever achieved greater fame than the Five. In the late 1940s and early 1950s they forged a front line that was the scourge of defences throughout Scotland.

Gordon Smith was first to arrive, recruited by manager Willie McCartney in April 1941. He was widely believed to have been on the brink of joining Hearts at the time. Willie Ormond signed from Stenhousemuir, Eddie Turnbull had come from the junior grades and Lawrie Reilly was a product of local Juvenile football. The last piece of the jigsaw puzzle was the promotion of Bobby Johnstone from reserve football to first team duties.

April 1949 was a red letter day for Scottish football, although no-one appreciated it at the time. The friendly between Hibernian and Nithsdale Wanderers at Sanquar heralded the birth of the 'Famous Five'. They marked the occasion with eight goals between them. In May 1949 they played together in another friendly, this time against an Irish FA XI in aid of the Ulster Memorial Building Fund at Windsor Park, Belfast. Hibs won 4-0 with the scorers Johnstone (2), Smith and Turnbull.

On 15 October 1949 the Five lined up at Easter Road for their first competitive match in Division 'A' of the Scottish League. Hibs beat Queen of the South 2-0, with Smith and Turnbull finding the net. Little did the 25,000 crowd know that so much more was to come. Hibernian only lost three games that season – twice to Hearts and

These pages: My only hat-trick in senior football for Edinburgh Select against Burnley at Easter Road in 1961. I'm jumping for joy after the first, particularly as Willie Bauld put me through. The second was a penalty as I slot the ball past Adam Blacklaw.
Two angles of the third as I manage to slip the ball under Blacklaw.

Hibernian's 'Famous Five': Gordon Smith, Bobby Johnstone, Lawrie Reilly, Eddie Turnbull and Willie Ormond.

once to Third Lanark – and finished runners-up to Rangers. For the third season in succession Gordon Smith was top League scorer, with 25 goals to his credit.

The Five came into their own in season 1950/51, reaching the League Cup final and the Scottish Cup semi-final, before losing on both occasions to Motherwell. They won the League, however, with Lawrie Reilly top scorer on 23 goals. Retaining the title the following year, Lawrie bagged 27 League goals in a season that saw Hibs pip Rangers by four points, and they established a record by collecting 96 goals in their 30 matches. In 1952/53 Hibs failed only on goal average to take the title for a third consecutive year; on goal difference, they would have won. The Five netted 92 goals, including Gordon Smith's 300th for the club. In the same season Lawrie bagged no fewer than six hat-tricks, including a four-goal burst against Motherwell.

In 1953 they were almost chosen to play for the Scottish League against the League of Ireland. The selectors chose Smith, Johnstone, Reilly, Turnbull and Ormond but baulked at making it an all-time Hibs line, preferring Jimmy Bonthrone of East Fife to Eddie Turnbull.

All five forwards accrued 100 goals for Hibernian and they were revered by Scottish football fans due to their skill, artistry and goalscoring achievements. The final match in which they played as a line was at home to Clyde in January 1955. Two goals up at one stage, Hibs eventually went down 3-2. It was the end of an era. On 1 March 1955 Bobby Johnstone was transferred to Manchester City for £22,000.

Lawrie Reilly was a legend of the game and rated among the top forwards in Scottish history. From 1946 to 1958 he scored 185 goals in 253 appearances and 22 goals in 38 games for Scotland. Lawrie retired at twenty-nine through injury, otherwise his record would have been even more daunting.

I was delighted to play for Hibernian at Lawrie's testimonial game in December 1958 against an International Select XI that included Bobby Johnstone. Tommy Docherty's thoughts in the media afterwards were much appreciated: 'The Doc predicts big things for young Gibson. Scotland's wing half predicts a big future for Davie Gibson, who played against him in last night's friendly at Easter Road. Allowing for the fact that he will not get such freedom in a competitive match, this boy looks promising. You can give a bad player all the room in the world and he will still be bad, but Gibson looked class in everything he did with the ball.'

In an open and entertaining match, the Select XI defeated us 9-3. However it was against a backdrop of icy rain that kept the crowd down, as did the refusal of the Scottish FA to allow Lawrie to play in his own testimonial on a technicality, as he had already retired. In 2005 a more enlightened SFA inducted Lawrie into the Scottish Hall of Fame.

I appreciate nothing beats playing this wonderful game, but sometimes you get the opportunity to play with and meet a genius. Gordon Smith was definitely a genius and an idol for a generation of post-war fans. I believe he is still the only player to have won a Scottish League Championship with three different clubs – Hibs, Hearts and Dundee – and was capped 19 times by Scotland.

I first met Gordon when I was seventeen years old. I knew of him as a kid when he played against my team, Hearts. While playing for the enemy, I still admired his grace as a flying right-winger. Fourteen years later I was getting changed alongside him for my professional debut against Falkirk. Was I dreaming? During the next few years I fully realised how good a player he was. Supporters gave him the nickname of 'Gay Gordon' or 'The Prince of Wingers' and he was the only person I played with to call me 'David' as opposed to 'Davie'.

Gordon was one of the first footballers to travel abroad for his holidays. He drove a Porsche down to the south of France, became friends with Brigitte Bardot and was even an extra in the Hitchcock movie *To Catch a Thief*, filmed on the French Riviera in 1954. When he arrived at the start of the season, handsome and tanned, Gordon looked like a Greek god. When he arrived at the hotel for lunch before the game, his dress attire was nothing short of elegant – jacket and trousers, white silk shirt and tie and slip-on moccasins. We had never seen anything like it before – short back and sides, just under 6 feet tall with a smile to match, he was better looking than Cary Grant. A class act in so many ways, but above all he had time to encourage all the young players who wanted to listen. It was a sad day when Gordon left Hibs for Hearts after seventeen years but I feel very privileged to have played with him and, more importantly, to have known one of the true greats of Scottish football.

Alex Young was a likeable footballer. By that I mean even the opposition supporters enjoyed his elusive and elegant movement. His touch was sublime and delicate, a joy to watch. He caressed rather than kicked the ball and, while not physically powerful

The Hearts squad including Willie Bauld, Gordon Smith and Alex Young that won the Scottish League in 1960. Back row: McLeod (assistant trainer), Kirk, Marshall, Brown, Blackwood, Cumming, McFadzean, Higgins, Bauld, Harvey (trainer). Front row: Smith, Young, Milne, Crawford, Hamilton, Murray, Thomson, Bowman.

in the manner of a Dave Hickson or Tommy Lawton, he was still majestic in the air. Nor was Alex blessed with extreme pace but appeared to glide when others merely ran, giving basis to the legend that he would 'drift' back to Olympia instead of driving home after the match. I signed for Hibs long before the 1960 New Year's Day derby game against Hearts, which I didn't play in. However my feelings for the Hearts since my childhood days were still loyal. At inside forward to 'King' Willie Bauld was Alex and, as it was just after Xmas, carols were still being sung as he scored a brilliant hat-trick. It really did bring a lump to my throat when the supporters started singing 'Hark the Herald Angels sing, glory to our newborn king'. Alex became one of the best footballers of his time with Hearts.

Eleven months later Alex was snapped up by Everton and over the years in England I played against the 'Golden Vision' many times – he was richly gifted and always a class act. When we played at Goodison Park in November 1965 Alex was on the bench. We were leading 2-0 with goals from Jimmy Goodfellow and Jackie Sinclair when the Tannoy sparked into action. The speaker announced, 'There's an S.O.S. for a Mr Young.' The 30,000 Everton fans were onto it in a flash. 'About bloody time' was the echo around the stadium. Typical Scouse humour, even the players had to laugh. A

My Army pal Jim Baxter in Rangers colours, being chased by one of the 'Terrible Trio', Jimmy Wardhaugh, albeit after his transfer from Hearts to Dunfermline.

supporter called Mr Young had gone to the game and forgotten to leave the car keys for his wife.

As already mentioned, I first met up with 'Slim Jim' Baxter in the British Army football team. Jim was already a mega-star with Glasgow Rangers and Scotland, while I was plodding away with my inferiority complex in Hibs' reserve team. Playing with Jim or Private J. Baxter of the Black Watch Battalion during the tour of the Far East changed all that. Some of his arrogance rubbed off on me so much that, by the end of the tour, I was focused and confident I could make it in the English First Division.

Whoever or whatever Jim faced on a football field, he always thought he was the best and most of the time he proved it. Playing against England in 1963 at Wembley, Scotland won a penalty. 'Stand back,' shouted Jim, 'that's mine.' To crown his day, he also scored Scotland's other goal in a famous 2-1 victory. Later that year, playing for the Rest of the World against England, again at Wembley, Jim was alongside two of the greatest footballers the world has ever seen, Ferenc Puskás and Alfredo di Stefano. He was completely unfazed – his favourite shout when he wanted the ball was 'Gees it'. Jim demanded the ball all the time and the two greats were happy to pass to him. He was a genius with an unbelievable belief in his own ability. When Rangers played Celtic in the Scottish Cup final one year, the papers carried a story that Jim was injured and may miss the match. On the day of the final, when the Rangers bus arrived at Hampden Park, Jim walked across the corridor to the Celtic dressing room, opened the door and shouted, 'I'm playing boys!' A loud groan was heard from the Celtic players. If that's not arrogance, I don't know what is.

Of course there was the other side of Jim, especially when he'd downed a few Bacardis. After the Norway international in Bergen mentioned earlier that we threw away, we all went out for a few drinks to a bar then moved on to a night club. The curfew was about 11 p.m., by which time most of the guys were back in the hotel sitting around a table. Jim then walked in shouting the odds – 'Who the f***g hell threw a pint at me in the club?' He went round the table pointing the finger at each one of us. When he did that to Frank McLintock, my pal replied, 'Do that again and I'll put you through that f***g window!' He finally got round to the smallest guy around the table apart from me, Willie Henderson, his team-mate at Rangers. Willie could pack a punch and was up for it but Jimmy Millar, another club-mate who was sitting next to Willie, quietly said, 'Hey Jim, think it's time for you to go to bed.' He'd also had some pretty uncomplimentary words with Willie Allan, the secretary of the Scottish FA and a powerful force behind the scenes, who was seated at the other end of the table. Allan was horrified with Jim's behaviour and we thought he might be sent home, but he survived to fight another day.

Another legend was Dave Mackay. I remember him well from his days as a young and aggressive wing half for Hearts. I played with Dave in the Scotland friendly match at Ibrox in 1959 – he'd just been transferred to Tottenham for £29,999, the bargain of a lifetime. When Spurs visited Leicester at Filbert Street in March 1963, imagine my surprise when walking out I met Dave in the tunnel. He stuck out his hand, welcomed me and handed out a card. My first thought was what a lovely gesture until I opened it and found a menu card for the local hospital that night – typical Mackay humour.

My old team-mate at Leicester Richie Norman was physio at Derby when Dave was manager. A friendly was arranged between a Nottingham Combined XI and Loughborough Students. In the first minute the ball came out to the young right-winger. He flew down the wing like all young men do, past Dave then Richie, crossed the ball and the centre-forward headed the ball into the net. Richie said to Dave, who was over forty at the time, 'It looks like we're in for a pounding today.' Typically, Dave responded, 'The game isn't over yet.' The next time the winger went on a run Mackay deposited him over the surrounding ropes. He never thought of running down the wing again and the old boys went on to win the match. I remember saying to Richie, 'Do you ever wonder why Tottenham won the 'Double' and we didn't?' He was one of the greatest professionals in my time as a footballer.

This poem about Dave was penned by my pal Billy Hunter at a tribute dinner and called 'The Real Mackay'.

> You can talk all night of Zola, with those magic twinkling feet,
> Or hard man Dennis Wise, whose tough guy tackling makes ye' greet,
> Then there's 'pin-point-passing' Beckham, supreme among his peers,

The legendary Dave Mackay looks as though he is trying to make a serious point as I'm having some banter with that other great, Denis Law. Just behind is a serious-looking Jim Forrest as we arrive for training with Scotland.

Whilst we've Gazza with his box of tricks … and a crate of local beers.
You've Scholes of Man-United, who can also stretch the net,
Viera with his vision … and one we never can forget,
Eric Cantona, the genius, who invented impromptu,
A timely 'meg's', a swerving shot, and then the old Kung Fu.
In days of yore we'd Bremner, a little fireball of skill,
Jim Baxter, playing each game, like he was in Brazil,
Bobby Murdoch of the Celtic, who laid on goals galore,
Big Greggie's reign at Rangers, with his rare *esprit de corps.*
The mention of these superstars may have you asking 'Why?'
Quite simply … without dispute … we have the real Mackay!
The Marquis had all these qualities, and tonight we celebrate,
From Newtongrange to Tynie, down to London then Kuwait.
His spell at Derby County, when he played for Brian Clough,
And then became the manager … when Brian took the huff!
It all started back in '51, when the Jam Tarts signed him up.
They didn't realise, that soon, he'd help them win the Cup.
But first he went to Nitten, where the tough guys made him wince,
There were old pros, and some miners, with there heids all full o' mince.
Surviving that, in '53, the Jambos called him in,
They must have had a premonition … Dave's middle name was – WIN.
Alongside Johnny Cumming, Andy Bowman, Alec Young,
Freddie Glidden, Jimmy Murray … how the names roll off your tongue,
Willie Duff, and Kirk and Thomson, two footballing full-backs,
With Willie Bauld and Ian Crawford, they arrested cardiacs!
The Hearts then won the Scottish League, the League and Scottish Cup,
And at long last, gave the Hearts' loyal fans, the chance to have a sup.
But all good things come to an end, and Dave Mackay moved south,
When Tottenham, with their thirty grand, took him down to their goalmouth.
That spell with Spurs were Glory Years … and it isn't hard to guess,
That once again the Marquis was the mainstay of success.
The Hotspurs' 'push and run' style was the plan of old Bill Nick
With Greaves, and Smith, and our own John White, it all just seemed to click.
Although Dave had suffered two leg breaks, his move to Derby showed,
In this old dog there still was life … not yet Madame Tussauds!
Then finally, for 15 years, he roamed the desert sand.
He'd carved his name among the greats … Rob Roy to Genghis Khan.
For Dave Mackay, read Braveheart, a powerhouse de luxe,
When fights broke out, you'd find oor Dave, in the middle of the rucks.
His leadership, without a doubt, was Churchill at his best,
He could, because he had achieved, stick out that barrel chest.
And skill … let's see … even now he can … on his instep or his toe,
Catch a spinning coin, thrown in the air … don't bet … you'll lose your dough.
The goals he scored from left half-back, with boots submerged in glaur,

> A hat-trick in '57, the Bairns all screamed – 'No more!'
> Dave's passing too was unsurpassed, and whether long or short,
> 'Jest gies it back … its mine … no yours', the Marquis would retort.
> He had it all, of that I'm sure, and on this gala night,
> Let's toast our legend … Dave Mackay … our man is … outasight!

In January 1962 I first met my fellow Scot Frank McLintock and, over fifty years on, we are still the best of friends. It was a sad day for me when he was transferred to Arsenal, where he became a Highbury legend. Frank scored 25 goals in 168 appearances for the Foxes over seven years at Filbert Street, forging a celebrated half-back partnership with Colin Appleton and Ian King. Frank was an excellent footballer at Leicester, but it was at Arsenal that he really made his mark and matured into a great player. It was a stroke of genius when Gordon Clark, the chief scout, suggested to Don Howe that Frank could be a better centre half than wing half. He led them to the Inter-Cities Fairs Cup final in 1969/70, defeating Anderlecht 4-3 on aggregate. The following year he skippered Arsenal to the Football League and FA Cup 'Double', the first time in the club's illustrious history. To cap it all, he won the coveted Football Writers' Association Player of the Year award in 1971. Frank had that special ingredient that made him stand out from the rest, a combination of toughness and never-say-die spirit, a determination to be a leader and winner in common with Dave Mackay. Nine appearances for Scotland was scant reward for his undoubted talents.

Away from football Frank's other passion was golf, which was on the horizon at Leicester every Monday, our day off. City had arranged for us to be able to play at Rothley Golf Club, a few miles from Anstey, where Frank's mother-in-law lived. A few months into the season, while visiting her on a Friday afternoon, Frank fancied playing a few holes with me. When I protested that club rules stated we couldn't play golf after Wednesdays, Frank assured me nobody would see us. When did I ever win an argument with Frank? We made our way untroubled to the fifteenth green when, looking across the fairway over the brook towards the first green, I was horrified to spot Matt Gillies playing. Panic set in rather quickly as we left our clubs at the side of the green, climbed over the fence into the brambles and bushes, and hid like two scared kids. What happened to the rough, tough Scotsman I played with? Frank came out with the classic, 'Do you think he's seen us? We can see him.' We waited until Matt and his partner played the second, then drove over the hill at the third and disappeared. Eventually we came out of the bushes and finished the game.

The next day – 13 October 1962 – we played Liverpool at Filbert Street. Sitting in the dressing room, Matt walked in at two o'clock. 'Everyone okay?' he enquired. 'Fine boss,' we all replied. 'Good luck and do your best,' and left the room. Frank looked over to me with a big smile on his face – he can't have seen us. Fortunately we won 3-0 and I waded in with the third goal. Picture the scene in the dressing room afterwards, laughing and shouting after a wonderful result, when in walked the manager. He went round the players congratulating them and finally came and sat between Frank and I. 'You were both terrific,' and as he turned to walk away, added, 'Oh by the way, you two can play golf every Friday!'

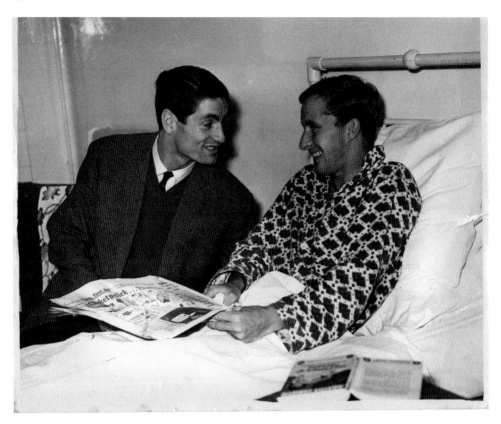

Recuperating in hospital after having my tonsils removed. My great pal Frank McLintock is cheering me up.

At the beginning of 1964 Frank and I had an idea of renovating the area underneath the stand and putting a licensed bar in for the supporters and players to use. The club wasn't so keen and when I went to Scotland during the summer, in order to give us a bit of leverage I said I wasn't going to sign a new contract, but didn't ask for a transfer. I didn't want to move, it wasn't my style, I loved it at Leicester and after all we had a great team. The club wouldn't agree to our idea though and nothing came of it. Within a year or two of course every club in the country put bars in the stadium. When I look at the fantastic players' facilities now, in the 1960s we had the smallest room you could imagine at Filbert Street, where about twenty-four bottles of beer were brought in for us to drink after the game.

On conclusion of the 1963/64 season, we embarked on a short tour of Austria. One of the 'friendly' matches was at Innsbruck against Linz. After an uneventful opening half-hour Frank was back defending, chasing the left-winger. As Frank tried to get close to him, the winger's arms were flying all over the place and his elbow smacked Frank on the nose. Now when Frank felt pain he turned into a monster and in the split second he felt the blow he exploded. The winger stumbled and fell, Frank followed through and kicked him in the face, smashing his teeth and bursting his nose. With blood all over his shirt, players from both sides arrived quickly on the crime scene. The first to confront Frank was their centre forward. They stood eyeballing each other for about two seconds when this fella gave Frank the 'Glasgow Kiss', a full-on head-butt. For a moment I thought Frank was down and out. Well he did go down, about 3 inches, and found a right-hook that Joe Louis would have been proud of. Plumb on the forward's chin, what a knock-out. All the other Linz players who had been trying to get close to Frank stopped in their tracks as Frank, his shirt covered in blood, turned round and shouted, 'Who's f***g next?' The ref stepped in, got hold of Frank and sent him off. They actually had to carry off the centre forward. As Frank was escorted from the pitch by Alex Dowdells with a sponge over his nose, he asked him, 'What will happen to me now?' Alex replied, 'Don't worry son, we're in N.A.T.O.' Some friendly. Frank reminded me of John Wayne that afternoon – he was always keen on cowboys.

Over the years Frank and I, together with our wives Mavis and Barbara and the children, have shared holidays in places such as Devon, Cornwall, Isle of Wight, Spain and Portugal. Once the children had flown the nest, it was just the four of us, travelling to wonderful destinations like Australia, South Africa and Singapore. Unfortunately I only played a couple of years with Frank at Leicester and can honestly say they were the best two seasons of my career. It was a pleasure to play with him for that short time but an even greater pleasure to call him a friend for over fifty years. Even though we argue every time we are in each other's company, I wouldn't have it any other way.

I also had the privilege of playing with three great goalkeepers, but even they had embarrassing moments in their careers.

Firstly Ronnie Simpson, who was transferred to Hibernian in 1960, a veteran of over 350 games with Queens Park, Third Lanark and Newcastle United. Approaching the veteran stage, United sold Ron to Hibs and were relegated that season. Coincidence or not, I wonder. Ron became a regular at Hibernian for the next four seasons, notching up another 123 matches. I was fortunate to play with Ronnie on a number of occasions, including the 1961 Fairs Cup semi-final when we lost to Roma.

After training one day I quizzed him, 'How do you work out which way to dive when facing a penalty kick?' Ron replied, 'First of all which foot does the taker kick with? If it is with his right foot, he will tend to shoot across himself, i.e. to the goalkeeper's right, and a left-footer the opposite.' I was still just a youngster and that advice came in handy the following season, during the Burnley charity match mentioned earlier. When we were awarded the penalty kick our captain Willie Bauld called me over – 'Ok son, its yours.' As I stepped forward to place the ball on the spot, I looked up and there stood Adam Blacklaw. Somehow Adam had got a great deal bigger in those last few seconds, but my little football brain clicked into gear and I remembered what Ronnie had told me. Do all goalkeepers think the same, I momentarily wondered, but my mind was made up. I hit it as hard as I could with my left foot, not to Adam's left but the opposite corner, and scored. The relief was palpable.

In 1964 a new manager arrived at Easter Road, Mr Jock Stein. By now Ronnie was thirty-three and within weeks Jock transferred him to Glasgow Celtic. Amazingly, in 1965 the same manager who sold Ronnie to Celtic took over at Parkhead. Ronnie probably thought that would be the end of his career, but under Jock he won international caps, League titles, League Cups and was ultimately inducted into the Scottish Hall of Fame. Of course he also became a legend in 1967 as the elder statesman of the Lisbon Lions, when Celtic won the European Cup. I couldn't believe it when Milan were awarded a penalty after just six minutes. Remembering his advice to me, what would Ronnie do? He took off his cap, tossed it into the net and, as Sandro Mazzola shot with his right foot to Ron's right, Ron dived to his left, 1-0. Well, as it was seven years later and Ronnie was now thirty-seven years young, I think we can forgive him.

Next the great Gordon Banks, 'Banksie'. In April 1965 we were scheduled to play at Tottenham. Leaving Filbert Street by bus, it was pouring with rain and never stopped until we reached White Hart Lane. The rain was relentless – all we witnessed was a

Johnny MacLeod tosses a coin into the Trevi Fountain in Rome. Ronnie Simpson and I are watching. We returned to Rome, only to get hammered 6-0 by Roma.

Living the high life in Rome, 1961, hopefully after the match: Eddie Turnbull, Tommy Preston, Ronnie Simpson, Joe McClelland, John Fraser, John MacLeod, myself and Eric Stevenson.

sea of wet mud, so there was understandably a pitch inspection. The referee came out with boots on and ball in his hand. He dropped the ball, it plopped on the mud and stayed there. He took a short run down the wing, tried to dribble the ball and it stuck in the mud. He declared the match on – we couldn't believe it. Within a few minutes all the players were covered in you know what. It certainly didn't suit our style of play and, with ten minutes remaining, we were trailing 5-2 when Tottenham were awarded a penalty kick. Gordon came storming out of his goalmouth – 'Referee, look at the conditions, nobody can keep their feet, no-one can stand up.' It made no difference, so Gordon turned and made his way back to his goalmouth. As his gloves were also covered in mud he knelt down in the corner of the goal, the only place where there was any grass and started cleaning his gloves. Who is waiting to take the penalty, the one and only Jimmy Greaves. With Gordon squatting in one corner, Jimmy coolly tapped it into the other. On hearing the whistle Gordon looked up to see all the Spurs players making their way back to the halfway line. Gordon ran through the mud and caught up with the referee – 'You can't be f***g serious, first of all it wasn't a f***g penalty, second you could see I was cleaning my f***g gloves and thirdly, surely you could see I wasn't f***g ready.' By now all the players within earshot were pissing themselves with laughter and I'm certain that saved Gordon from being sent off. The ref waited until Gordon had finished then quietly said, 'Mr Banks I was ready, Mr Greaves was ready, the whole stadium was ready, I had given a penalty and I have given a goal. If you don't get back in your goalmouth, you will be having an early bath.' Poor old Gordon had to turn, covered in mud and plod his way back to the goalmouth – you couldn't make it up.

Thirdly Peter Shilton, who made his debut at the age of sixteen on 4 May 1966 against Everton, a 3-0 win and a clean sheet. Moving forward to March 1968, when we played Sheffield United at Filbert Street. They gained an early corner on the left wing and Alan Woodward, their right-winger, a wonderful crosser of the ball, came over to the left. John Sjoberg was standing at the near post. Woodward's cross came in like a bullet and Peter Shilton cried, 'Leave it.' John ducked and at that speed the ball hit Peter and cannoned into the net. On the Monday morning Bert Johnson was going over the game and of course that goal was the main topic of conversation. 'What have I always preached?' implored Bert. 'The first defender in a position to clear the ball, clear it, clear the danger.' Peter wasn't happy with Bert's opinion. 'That's great,' said Peter, 'I'm coming out and shout leave it, the defender doesn't, I collide with him and we both go tumbling to the ground.' 'So long as the ball hasn't landed in the net, that's okay by me,' replied Bert. Peter had the last word – 'That will never happen in a million years.'

Two weeks on, we played at Nottingham Forest and I recall a long ball into our penalty area. John Sjoberg was waiting to head clear when he heard a shout of 'Leave it.' John had forgotten Bert's words to clear it and ducked again. Out of nowhere arrived Joe Baker, my old Hibs mate, who nipped in between Peter and John, got the faintest of touches and the ball finished in the back of our net. Standing on the half way line, I remembered those famous last words of young Peter, 'It will never happen in a million years!'

Two great keepers, Peter Shilton and Gordon Banks, inseparable in my opinion.

Two 'greats' of British football, Lawrie Reilly and Tom Finney.

Bill Shankly once said, 'Tom Finney would have been great in any team, even if he was wearing an overcoat.' Bobby Moore commented, 'If you were as good as Tom, you didn't have to tell anyone.' Sir Alex Ferguson said, 'He's such a wonderful person and so humble, why can't we all be like that?' In August 1957 Preston North End were the English team invited to play in the annual match against the Edinburgh Select XI at Easter Road. Tom was on the right wing, at thirty-five a veteran and some people might have claimed past his best, but don't you believe it. The young full-back marking him that day was George Muir, the oldest twenty-year-old you will ever see. Hugh Shaw was the Select manager and his team talk went something like this – 'Now young George, this old man on the right wing, don't be fooled by his age, he can still play a bit. When you tackle him and I mean tackle, you hit him hard.' George replied, 'But if I hit him that hard, he'll be carried off but I'll be sent off.' 'That's okay son, but they will miss him more than we'll miss you.' Preston won the match 3-1 and, like many full-backs over the years, George never got near Tom, who was awarded Man of the Match.

George Muir could kick his granny. When I first joined Hibs as a kid I saw this big, strapping lad with fair hair. He was a schoolboy international, but to a wee lad like me he looked about thirty-five. I played a few times with George, but he went on his National Service, was posted at Houndstone Camp in Yeovil and never came back. He became a bit of a cult hero with Yeovil Town, playing over 300 times for the club and I later caught up with him at a pub close to Yeovil to reminisce about the old days.

18

And Finally…

When, why and how did football all go wrong in Britain? Why do we always fail in the big tournaments? Could it be the weather? No, it also rains in Spain and Germany. Could it be the pitches? No, the football pitches the world over are top class. What about the ball, the boots, the gloves or the strips? No, they are universal. Does it boil down to how we are taught as children? Possibly, although Stanley Matthews and Tom Finney were never coached as kids. Does it come down to size and strength? On that point some of the finest players I have ever seen were Puskás, Kopa, Johnstone, Pele, Tostao, Gerson, Maradona, Scholes, Messi, Iniesta and Xavi. What did they have in common? They were all under 5 feet 9 inches and very comfortable on the ball. Could that be the secret?

A question I've been asked many times is whether or not the standard of British football is higher than it was forty years ago. Is football a better product now, do supporters get more value for money now, paying £50 compared with two bob? Undeniably the stadiums and facilities are now magnificent, the ball is lighter and travels a long way in the air, the goalkeepers wear better gloves, the strips are more colourful, the boots are all the colours of the rainbow, the crowds are more aggressive and segregated, the tactics and formation can be confusing and defensive, but do they all add up to a superior product in the field? I'm not so sure. In my eyes football was more entertaining after the war and up to the end of the 1970s. In today's game, if you are fortunate enough to see a goal or witness a quality pass, television will play it over and over again – they have to, as you may not see another one in the entire ninety minutes. Can you believe it can take about two minutes to plan and execute a free kick or even a throw in – is that progress? How can it be more exciting when teams play with one forward? If we use a simple rule of thumb to describe entertaining football, i.e. scoring more goals than the opposition, then surely the game as we know it has gone backwards.

Try telling me that players are quicker now than in the past. Talk to defenders who tried to catch John Connelly of Burnley or Cliff Jones of Tottenham. Or to Joe Baker – they were all flying machines. I would concede the game is now faster, but when I played more players stopped the ball, caressed it, passed it then wanted it back. Great examples were Johnny Haynes of Fulham, Jimmy McIlroy of Burnley, Bryan Douglas of Blackburn and that great entertainer Charlie Cooke of Chelsea.

Prior to the advent of more defensive tactics, Malcolm MacDonald, Andy Gray, Andy Lochhead and further back Tommy Lawton, Nat Lofthouse, Arthur Rowley and Stan Mortensen regularly scored hat-tricks, producing headers among the flying boots. Where have all the flying wingers gone, with their variety of tricks that came in all different sizes and shapes? Some were quick, quick, slow, others ran like the wind, all because they had a number 7 or 11 on their shirt. Their job was to deliver the ammunition into the penalty area without fail or else the artistry would have been all for nothing. The winger was a creature of beauty, a golden eagle when in full flight, but has been replaced by overlapping wing-backs or wide midfield players, which doesn't feel quite the same to me. How can this type of player bear favourable comparison with Stanley Matthews, Tom Finney, Jimmy Johnstone, George Best, Garrincha or Willie Henderson?

Certain coaches and managers in my opinion have taken their responsibilities too far. Until they take a step back and allow players the freedom to express themselves, I can't see a British nation being successful in future major competitions. I'm not against talking and educating a youngster up to the age of, say, twenty, but if you haven't grasped it by then, you're highly unlikely to beyond that age. Once the game starts, let them play how they feel. It may help if you are born with a football brain, while some make it to the top through grit and determination. I don't think George Graham ever coached Ian Wright at Arsenal – he let him express himself and score goals. However, he coached and disciplined his team how to play when the opposition had the ball. He made his opponents play to his strengths and Arsenal were brilliant at it.

Years ago you had a manager who picked the team, a trainer who got all the players fit and a physio who got all the players fit again, for example Alf Ramsey, Les Cocker and Harold Shepherdson... and they won the World Cup. Alf changed his line-up during the finals, that's what managers should do, but he didn't shout and bawl at his players from the first to last minute, like some do now. When will they realise that not one player is listening, as they are too engrossed in the game? The great managers of the past – Busby, Stein, Clough, Paisley, Ramsey, Nicholson – had wonderful players in abundance. Their motto was attack is the best form of defence. They found or bought the best players and moulded them into winners.

Enough of my views – I mentioned earlier how this wonderful game can turn many a manager's head. Here are a few quotes to illustrate my point;

'He's got two arms and two legs and when he finds his feet he'll be brilliant.' Ian Porterfield when signing Charlie Nicholas for Aberdeen.
'What makes a good manager? To keep the six players who hate you away from the five who are undecided.' Jock Stein.
'Do you sleep well at night?' 'I sleep like a baby. I wake up crying four times a night.' John Duncan.
'Mortensen was that good they named the Cup final after him. The Stanley Matthews final.' Lawrie McMenemy.

'I've seen Desert Orchid fall, I've seen George Best refuse a drink, I've even seen Emlyn Hughes buy a drink so anything is possible.' Alan Ball.

'I'm not superstitious but hope we play at our best and put it in the lap of the Gods.' Terry Neill.

'The last time we got a penalty kick Jesus Christ was a carpenter.' Lennie Lawrence.

'Be careful the toes you stand on today may be connected with the arse you have to kiss tomorrow.' Tommy Docherty.

I also chuckle at some of the imaginative one-liners about me the press boys came up with;

'The blond whippet with the educated feet.'

'His legs worked like a pair of super-fast knitting needles.'

'He is a finely balanced player of rapid decisions and even quicker action, with an almost lyrical style.'

'Leicester's explosive bundle of T.N.T.'

'Gibson, as great a masterpiece of ingenuity as a Persian miniature.'

'The impish inside left with impeccable control.'

'Silky skills even though a strong gust of wind would have taken him out of sight.'

The late Alan Hoby, the voice of *Sunday Express* sport for thirty-seven years, wrote possibly the greatest compliment I ever had:

There's a haunting magic, a universal allure about a great footballer especially if he is a forward. Whisper his name and people become bewitched. Talk of his tricks, his foot flair, his conjurer's art and suddenly the skin prickles, the senses stir. Such were Alex James, Ferenc Puskás, Stanley Matthews, Denis Law, Jimmy Greaves and John White. But now up in the Midlands the hard-headed citizens of these parts are raving about an inside forward from Scotland who they swear is as good as, if not better than John White. Davie Gibson is the name and I suggest that all you football fans who live outside the city of Leicester mark it well. At the rate this laddie is going, it will soon be up there in big bold headlines along with the rest.

Thanks Alan – I might have been good and I'm sure you were sincere when you wrote it, but that was some company to be in. I was 5 feet 7 inches tall, 10 stone 4 pounds soaking wet, couldn't tackle, was hopeless in the air, not very quick and my right leg was just for standing on, but somehow I made it as a professional footballer.

Where else could I finish my story – my voyage of dreams? I've a lifetime of memories and my thanks to all the wonderful people I met along the way. Maybe I didn't win any League titles, FA Cups or World Cup medals, but I don't regret a moment other than that throw-out from Banksie in the Cup final. I'm very proud to be included in the Players' Hall of Fame display in the directors' lounge at Leicester. I'm grateful to John Hutchinson at City for organising the display of some of my Scotland memorabilia at the stadium. Also a special mention to Chris Westcott for his help and support in bringing this book together.

I had the most wonderful thirty-five years as a footballer, including my time with Birch's geriatrics at Leicester, from a kid in Winchburgh to playing for Scotland. I was fortunate to play in two FA Cup finals and two League Cup finals. I played at some of the greatest stadiums in the world: Hampden Park, Glasgow; Wembley; Dalymount Park, Dublin; Windsor Park, Belfast; Bernabéu Stadium, Madrid; Olympic Stadium, Rome; Old Trafford; White Hart Lane; Highbury; Parkhead; Ibrox; and of course Filbert Street.

Most footballers play for the challenge of competing, testing one's skills against the next man, the laughs and despairs of losing, but anticipation of the next game. Was it worth giving up the day job to test my skills on the football field? Yes, of course, and I would do it all again … for nothing.

Mavis and I enjoying retirement at home in 2013.

Tribute Section

Heart of Midlothian

Alex Young

I remember the derby game Davie mentioned at Easter Road in 1960. The record books showed me scoring a hat-trick, but I actually got four in the 5-1 win. The officials gave one as an own goal and wouldn't overturn it. Leicester were a very difficult team to beat when I was at Everton. Davie was a very good player and caused us a lot of trouble in midfield. I put him in the same bracket as Denis Law, Jim Baxter, George Best and Charlie Cooke. They were all capable of making a game remembered long after the result stopped being important. Davie was a nice, good-looking guy and I seem to recall all the girls fancied him with his blonde hair.

Hibernian

Jim Easton

I was just a young guy in my first season and lucky enough to get into the team when we played the European games. It was one of the reasons I joined Hibs – they also regularly went on tours to Europe.

I remember the two Fairs Cup legs against Barcelona in 1961, which Davie didn't play in. Our big name was Joe Baker – Eddie Turnbull said he would be a marked man, so he changed jerseys in the first tie with Tommy Preston. The opposition knew his number but wouldn't recognize his face, as they'd never seen him. Joe scored twice and we came away with a 4-4 draw in Barcelona, which was unbelievable as they had some top-class players. They'd just put Real Madrid out of the European Cup as at the time you could play in both tournaments. It was a real eye-opener to us out there. We'd never seen a dressing room with a huge Roman sunken bath before and they gave us red-and-white robes to wear. We all thought they would be a nice souvenir to come home with, but the equipment manager who handed them out told us they self-destructed twenty minutes after they left the dressing room!

The return leg at Easter Road was a debacle. It was 2-2 when we were awarded a penalty with about five minutes to go. I was at the other end of the field, but the Barcelona players were outraged and a riot broke out. Bobby Kinloch was at the other end of the pitch practising penalties on his own, cool as a cucumber, and when play finally resumed he slotted the ball exactly where he had been practising. Then they kicked anything that moved and completely lost the plot. They wrecked the dressing room and the Barcelona chairman wrote an open letter the next day and apologized for their behaviour.

We had to wait until April to play Roma in the semi-final. After a draw at Easter Road, we were winning 3-1 in Rome with less than ten minutes to go when the heavens opened. I'd never seen rain like that in my life, we just couldn't play and they came back to 3-3. There was no toss of the coin to decide the venue of the play-off – Harry Swan said we'd come back to Rome. He struck a deal for us to return for a week as long as they picked up the tab. It was more like a holiday for him and the directors! They agreed but Swan forgot to put a date on it, so Roma were shrewd enough to wait until our season had finished. We hadn't trained for a couple of weeks immediately before we returned and got beaten 6-0. To play at the Olympic Stadium in Rome was a dream. I wondered more than once what I was doing playing there – I should have been watching it!

I was playing directly against Manfredini and their players wanted to swap jerseys at the end of the match. We were told not to as the club needed them – we were the poor relatives and it was embarrassing for us. Manfredini could speak a bit of English and when I explained he took the Roma crest off his jersey and gave it to me – a great souvenir for me.

A year later and we played another top European side, Red Star Belgrade. On our way out we spent the night at Zurich because of fog and flew the next day to Belgrade. We were on the pitch getting ready to play, warming up, when Sekularac came out on his own. It was like the appearance of the Pope – he ran round the pitch waving at the spectators. We all thought, who does he think he is? As soon as we started to play we knew. After about twenty minutes the floodlights went out. We were in the game up to then – after that it was a runaway. In the second half Sekularac came through and went over the ball into our right-back Joe Davin, who was screaming in pain. He got a bad one down his shins. I was next in line and decided I wasn't going to have that, so I tackled him and you would think someone had shot Sekularac from the terraces. He rolled about for ten minutes – it wasn't that bad, but the referee came over and sent me off. Sekularac was screaming behind the referee and before I left the pitch he scratched me in the face. He wasn't a big guy and as soon as I touched him there was bedlam. I was standing toe to toe with the Red Star players and the next thing I knew Sammy Baird, who had been on the bench, was standing beside me. I walked towards a covered tunnel behind the goal, where there was a soldier with a machine gun smiling at me. He didn't allow me in but directed me to the stand and when I got there the supporters were spitting down onto me.

At the banquet after the game I found myself sitting right opposite Sekularac! He was such a big star but so arrogant and said (but not in English) that Di Stefano was the best player in the world and he was the second best. He never made an attempt to speak English and had so much power he didn't even bother to travel for the return leg in Edinburgh a couple of weeks later. I understand he even had to be coaxed to play for Yugoslavia in the 1962 World Cup finals.

Davie was a really good player. We didn't make a lot of money at Hibs but have memories that will stay with us for the rest of our days.

John MacLeod

I was an Edinburgh lad so the 'Famous Five' were my boyhood heroes, and Willie Ormond and Gordon Smith the two Hibernian wingers when I joined the club. Willie helped me a lot and 'Gay Gordon' was an immaculate chap who kept himself in really good shape.

My career went on a parallel with Joe Baker to a certain extent when we were both at Armadale Thistle for a couple of years. However, Davie and I did our National Service, but Joe didn't and in footballing terms it probably put me a bit behind Joe, who broke into the Hibs first team before me. I have no regrets whatsoever in doing my National Service as, like Davie, I would have been playing football pretty well every day of the week. The downside was some guy would be trying to kick me every day of the week, as I was connected to a League club. We had a few sprint competitions and while I was quicker than Joe off 10–15 yards, Joe could beat me over a longer distance.

I had a very bad experience with Harry Swan. He called me to an Edinburgh hotel in 1959 and tried to sell me to Luton, who were a good team and had reached the FA Cup final. They had seen me play when I was in the Royal Air Force down South. Swan said if I went there he would look after me, but threatened that if I didn't sign for them I'd never play for Hibs again. It didn't matter to me what he did or said, I didn't want to go, and the Luton manager and directors were very surprised at my decision. Swan also threatened to play me once on the left wing instead of the right – it was all very intimidating for a teenager as he was known to be such a powerful person in the game. There was always that in the background, so when Joe asked for a fiver-a-week rise and I asked for £2 a week at the end of the 1960/61 season, it was no great surprise that Swan refused and we were transferred. I'd just won my first international cap, so didn't think it an unreasonable request. If they'd made some movement I wouldn't have gone at all, as I was Hibs mad, and of course Joe and I were later reunited at Arsenal.

Davie was like a player's player, a very clever footballer who could see a pass and, with Hibs playing two wingers, he could release you early rather than others who may have lacked that level of awareness. He had a lovely left foot, could score goals and make goals. He was great at receiving a ball, you could fire the ball at him and he would bring it instantly under control, very much a one-touch player, then could thread me a pass – it was a dream for me as a winger. Bobby Johnstone was a hard act to follow, but Davie was a different type of player – he covered more ground than Bobby, who I only saw towards the end of his career.

After the 3-3 draw against Roma, Davie was voted Man of the Match by the players in the dressing room. He had a great game, making one of the goals for Joe. Roma did exactly the same for deciding the play-off venue as in the previous round. The scores were level against Cologne, who returned to Rome and lost 4-1. We hadn't done any training before we flew back to Rome for our play-off. We were taken out in the evenings there as well, so it was no great surprise we were beaten comprehensively.

British Army

John Quinn
Davie was a very skilful player. It's right that I suffered in the sun on tour with the British Army team. We went to a beautiful little beach, I think it was in Singapore, swimming and sunbathing. We were told not to sunbathe but, daft as a brush, I ignored the advice. I burnt all the back of my shoulders and Davie sat up all night putting calamine lotion on them. I missed a game and learned my lesson quickly. The Army team was full of internationals and I wondered how I could get into the side, but it was good experience for me in my future career at Sheffield Wednesday. I've played golf regularly with Davie and Mick Kearns, who was also on that tour. We've kept in touch ever since those days, Davie is a smashing lad, a good storyteller and one of my best friends.

Leicester City

Colin Appleton
Matt Gillies brought the right players together, especially the Scots with his contacts north of the border. We all knitted together to make it a special time and I was proud to lead them on the pitch as captain. The success in the early 1960s arose as the backbone of the side was permanent – there weren't many changes with a smaller squad.

It was a great team effort and Davie was a very important part of the team. Even though he was slight in stature, he had a good attitude and was an essential part of the jigsaw. You didn't see the opposition dominate him, as his skill and ball control enabled him to deal with evading the tackles when they came in.

Gordon Banks
Davie was a fine player, our playmaker, with excellent control of the ball. His creativity in seeing opportunities to slot the ball through for the forwards to run on to made it very difficult for the opposition. Davie knew exactly when to put an inch-perfect 40-yard pass into Mike Stringfellow's path and Stringy could really shift. Davie was a very likeable lad, we were all good friends and got on very well with each other at Leicester.

I was keen to develop my game at the time, as were Davie and Frank McLintock. We'd do all the hard training and a bit of ball work as well in the mornings, but it didn't include a lot of actual shooting. So I asked if anyone wanted to come back in the afternoons to give me some shooting practice. Davie and Frank, being single lads, had the time to do it so they would come back and cross and belt balls at me from all angles. It helped us all, but from my point of view it improved my positional game and reactions. For example, I'd ask them to half-volley the ball at me from five yards, never telling me which side of the goal it was going.

The 1963 FA Cup semi-final against Liverpool at Hillsborough was one of my best performances. Liverpool were a real top outfit with some great players and very highly regarded. While we were a better-than-average side, we knew it was going to be a very difficult tie. They controlled the game and kept coming at us, but we defended brilliantly and, being in the semi and keeping a clean sheet in front of a capacity crowd, it gave me such a thrill for us to be through to the final. It was one of those days where everything went right and was the busiest goalkeeping game that I ever played.

Frank McLintock

Davie was a brilliant player, very similar to John White of Tottenham. I don't think people realise how good a player he was. He could pass the ball short or long, he had great vision and scored 60-odd goals as well, so it wasn't just playmaking for other people all the time. He had a good shot on him even though he was quite skinny, but could leather those heavy balls we played with in those days. He lacked the physique to out-muscle the opposition, so had to out-think them. Davie set the tempo at which we played, had a magnificent touch and gave the team great impetus. He could fire a ball between the full-back and the centre half, and was the best exponent of the short angled killer pass into the box I ever played with.

When Davie and Mike Stringfellow signed for Leicester, it changed the way we played. Mike liked to come short and draw the full-back in, allowing Davie to skilfully chip one over the top with a hint of backspin, into space for him to run onto. Mike was a brave, tall, winger who never complained if he didn't receive a perfectly weighted pass to his feet every time. You didn't often get the ball back from Mike but no matter – he had a tremendous shot and the pace and acceleration that frightens defenders. He scored goals from wide positions, was good in the air and ran all day in support of the team. Physically, the two players had nothing in common bar an uncanny understanding between them.

Davie has always been mad keen on his football, always trying to come up with new ideas for free-kicks, corner-kicks and even throw-ins. We must have been perfect for any coach or manager, as both of us were football nuts. If he had a fault it was his tendency to overdo the theory – 'You're too bloody clever by half', we used to tell him. In the Army he played alongside Jim Baxter, whose love of intricate dead-ball routines had rubbed off on him. Davie was always up to something and when we played at Bolton he devised this routine where three of us stood over the ball, but he and I would run over it and Bobby Roberts would play the ball in. When it came to it, Bobby and I were a bit confused and all three of us dummied and sprinted into the box, leaving no-one to take the kick. Roy Hartle, Bolton's tough full-back, glared at us and in his broad Lancastrian accent commented, 'Too many f***g cooks spoil t'broth lads!' On another occasion we were only about 10 yards out when we were awarded a free-kick. The opposition was lined up on the goal line and Davie came up with another complicated manoeuvre. I said, 'Just pass it to me and I'll batter it into the net.' And that's exactly what I did. I told him we didn't need to do that intricate stuff all the time, so we had a wee laugh about it.

When we weren't playing football we were always talking about it. Davie's a football fanatic and still talks tactics and players non-stop. If you have a drink with him he'll fire trivia questions at you all night. If I answer any question quickly, he'll always end up with a counter-argument. Whenever we go on holiday we finish up arguing all the time. We've known each other since our early twenties, when he joined Leicester, and hit it off from the start. It's continued that way for over fifty years now. I get on brilliantly with him and love him dearly.

Bobby Roberts

I've known Davie since he worked as a joiner in Edinburgh, playing part-time for Hibs, and I was playing for Motherwell reserves. Living at Abbeyhill in Edinburgh, sometimes Davie came round our house for something to eat before training. On Saturday night a crowd of four or five of us met up for the dancing at the Palais. There wasn't the range of clubs to go to like nowadays – the Palais was the only dance hall, so all the lads went there on a Saturday. We went on holiday together and had a good laugh and a few drinks in Jersey one year. We were always either playing football or talking about football with guys like Billy Hunter, Tommy Kilbride and Jim Robertson.

Davie was instrumental in me coming to Leicester in September 1963. I'd asked Motherwell for a transfer, but they wanted to sell me to Ipswich. Jackie Milburn, their manager, thought quite highly of me and they were offering me more wages than Leicester. I'd obviously known Davie for a while – he told me Leicester were interested and said the football was good, so I made my mind up to go there. Davie had just enjoyed a great first season with Leicester, and myself and Billy Hunter flew to London to watch the FA Cup final, confident of seeing a victory. Davie got us a couple of tickets and there was a fabulous atmosphere, but on the day United's class players played very well and the pitch suited them.

Davie had a great range of passes – he could knock them short, knock balls over the top of the full-back or play them inside people. If he found room and space in the middle of the park, he would hurt teams with his range of passes. When he got the ball on his left 'peg' he could really make it happen and scored a lot of goals too. The game used to be continuous, but the accent is now on passing the ball. The Continental influence to make sure teams perform better in Europe means a slower build-up. I've seen teams nowadays play the ball around twenty times but lack that killer pass. It used to be a more direct type of game and we were expected to go forward. If we passed it around as much as teams do now, we'd have been booed off the park. Derek Dougan, Allan Clarke or Andy Lochhead would have been screaming blue murder – they wanted the ball into the box as quickly as possible.

If you're a good player you can play in any era. Davie could easily play now – he would get more space and time on the ball than when we played. Davie passed it beyond people, with the skill to put just enough pace on the ball for the forward to run on to it. We enjoyed some good runs in the Cup and had a spell playing together in the middle of the park. We did work on some moves in training, wee throw-ins and free-kicks, but because we knew each other well we were on the same wavelength. My job was to get the ball, give it to Davie and he'd do the rest. He was quite quiet on the park, aside from a quick quip to the referee or opposition – he got on with his job and certainly did that well. We always had a laugh off the park – Davie's a great lad and was a pleasure to play with.

Mike Stringfellow
I joined Leicester at the beginning of 1962 and took over from Gordon Wills and John Mitten, who I was in digs at Highfields with for about three months until he was transferred to Coventry. Our paths had already crossed at Mansfield when I was in the youth team. John's father Charlie was the manager and John was in the first team. Then Charlie became manager at Newcastle and John followed, before joining Leicester. John was also a very good cricketer, a wicket-keeper, and played county cricket for Leicestershire in 1962/63.

I didn't have a problem with all the Scots at the club, but I had great difficulty in understanding some of them, most of all Alex Dowdells. They all called me 'Stringy', it was a nickname from my school days. My first memory of Davie was him flying in from the Army to play for us. We clicked straight away – it's quite amazing as we never practised anything and it wasn't coached, it just happened. Davie had an excellent first touch, was an accurate passer with good vision and also scored quite a few goals. He didn't get many injuries – he was too clever for that.

When I finished playing I ran an off-licence for about a year in the town and one day the postman walked in. Who should it be but Davie, my postman working at Earl Shilton post office!

The Cup semi-final goal against Liverpool in 1963 was not necessarily the best I scored but definitely the most important. The best was at Sheffield Wednesday a few years later in the League when I got the ball in my own half and went right through and scored.

Leicester & Aston Villa

Andy Lochhead
When I went to Leicester I met up with David and we played a couple of seasons together. He was always a great crosser of the ball. As a striker he made numerous goals for me the way he delivered the ball into the box. When I was transferred to Aston Villa, Vic, Crowe asked me if there was anyone at Leicester I would ideally like to bring with me. I told him if he could get Davie it would be tremendous. Vic made an enquiry and Leicester let Davie go. We had a good couple of seasons at Villa and were good friends. He had an excellent left foot, he'd go up to a defender, make the angle, dip his shoulder and whip the cross in. All I had to do was get to the near post to get a touch. Strikers like us relied on good service and Davie was one of the best crossers of the ball I ever played with.

Aston Villa

Leo Crowther (Coach)

Despite the fact that Davie was over thirty when he signed for us, he added so much to the Villa team. We had the powerhouse in Bruce Rioch and needed a touch person like Davie. As far as Ron Wylie and I were concerned, Davie was the player with the best touch we had at Villa. Whenever we had some coaching or exercises to perform, we always asked Davie to do it for us, as he had a magical left foot. Ron thought a lot of Davie, they had in common the Scottish ability to dribble and beat people, and Davie was also a very good trainer. He would be an ideal midfield player nowadays – he would have fitted in a treat.

When Davie just missed out for selection in the 1971 League Cup final, we ruminated over the options quite a lot, but felt the extra power of Bruce Rioch might count against a First Division team. We had a great youth team under Frank Upton and won the Youth Cup against Liverpool in 1972. Davie was always there if the youngsters needed a bit of advice and contributed to a very good spirit. We have kept in touch, even when Davie retired. He is such a lovely man with a lovely family.

Bruce Rioch

Davie and Andy Lochhead came along at a good time. I joined Villa in 1969 when Tommy Docherty was manager and when he left Vic Crowe and Ron Wylie took over. A lot of us were youngsters and the club suffered relegation in my first season when I was hoping we would go in the other direction. There had been a lot of changes at Villa in the previous twelve months, and Davie and Andy were two great signings. The impact they had was immense, as it was two key positions in the team. Together with Chris Nicholl, Ray Graydon and George Curtis, they came in and added experience to the team. Andy led the line and had a big influence on our style of play, as we had a focal point up front. You could play off him and Davie was the playmaker. Davie was great for the dressing room, effervescent like James Cagney, and it created a fantastic atmosphere. He could tell a tale, which is great to have at a football club, the mood and atmosphere was always bubbly. It was never quiet when Davie and Jimmy Cumbes were around. We had some great personalities, and to have that class and experience come in and help the young players like Chico Hamilton and Pat McMahon, plus Brian Little making his way through, was priceless.

Davie was a craftsman with talent, drive, desire, good awareness and anticipation. He was a clever player who could read the game and other people protected him, as it was quite physical at the time. He had an educated left foot and quick brain, was an organiser and always available to receive a pass. He wasn't short of fitness – we trained hard at Villa with Ron Wylie and he was in good shape.

We were different type of players – I was more offensive, Davie was a creator, sheer class, and the team did fantastic with him in the side instead of me. I damaged my knees during the previous season, which required surgery, and I had a double cartilage operation. I was still out for the first leg of the League Cup semi-final and watched us get a good result at Old Trafford. For me the second leg was the most memorable of all the games I can remember at Villa and I was only on the bench! There were 60,000 in the stadium, creating a wonderful atmosphere, and Davie's influence was immense. Davie was left out of the team for the final and, while I was happy to play, I think Davie should have stayed in and I've told him. He'd played at Wembley before and it was a stadium made for him. I know, having managed, I would have gone with the experience and ability of Davie, as he got us there. Perhaps it was in the light of losing the game, but deep down it would have been right for him to play because of his performances leading up to the final.

There was an abundance of top players in the Scotland side when Davie was playing, otherwise he would have won many more caps. He had a huge impact on me and we've become friends to this day, mainly meeting up nowadays on the golf course. When I played under Alex Stock at Luton, he told us in the dressing room to go out and play with class and style, and Davie did just that.

Exeter City

Alan Banks

We were very surprised when Davie arrived with his pedigree and experience, but it was great for us to have a class player like Davie in the side. He was slight but had tremendous ability on the ball, was a great character and terrific storyteller. When he was looking for a house in Exeter, I brought him down and he bought a house in our close, so we went into training together every day. When I was transferred to Poole Town in 1973/74, I took Davie's son Stuart and my own son with me to watch Poole.

One of the Exeter matches we played in together was April 1972, when we beat Barrow 7-1, which was their last ever game in the Football League. We had a great run during the early part of the 1972/73 season. Beating West Brom in the League Cup was a wonderful result but also from a financial point of view, and things haven't changed at Exeter to this day. There's a nucleus of players from Davie's time that go to every home game – we were all good friends and keep in touch. We talk about how good we were!

Campbell Crawford

We enjoyed a good season with Davie in the side – he found it fine to play at that level, but then we fell away. Perhaps a couple of bad results affected our confidence and our form. I enjoyed beating my old team West Brom in 1973, Fred Binney scored a couple of goals that night.

For most of our away games we stayed away on Friday and with matches at Harlepool, Darlington or Workington, it could be Tuesday before we arrived back in Exeter. We used to room together and of course Davie never stops talking. On a Friday night we would watch a late-night show on television like *Streets of San Fransisco* until it was time to switch the lights out. However, Davie would carry on taking football until one o'clock in the morning – not the best preparation for a match the next day!

Jimmy Giles

Davie was a character, bubbly on the training pitch, and always encouraged the young kids there. He'd played top-level football so we had a lot of respect for him, but he was just an ordinary down-to-earth bloke and we loved him to bits. At Southport on the opening day of the 1972/73 season, Davie came back to defend the near post, going up for it, and it came off his head and flew into the back of the net for the only goal of the game. I looked at him and all he said was, 'Oops.' After that I told him never to come back again! I used to look after him – if we were on the park and someone was kicking him, he'd come up and tell me. I'd have a quick chat with the fella kicking him to make sure it didn't happen again. I looked after him on and off the pitch because he was a tight bugger! He was not only a great footballer, a great crosser of the ball, but also very good in the dressing room. He always had something to say – we could never stop him talking and it's the same when you play golf with him. I'm not sure if you're going to have characters like Gibbo again, as the game's become so serious.

John Newman (Manager)

I had a call to mark my card that David was interested in moving to the West Country, so I contacted Aston Villa and they agreed subject to, I think, the enormous fee of about £5,000. Sometimes you sign footballers not only because they can play, but because they can also have an influence on other players. I always felt that David had a good influence and that became noticeable within a couple of weeks of signing. I knew of his reputation and what sort of lad he was. It was a pleasure for me to watch David and Tony Scott in particular perform. We had a good side, but we just missed out on promotion. It would have been to their credit but we couldn't quite finish it off. I always blame them not me!

David came to me a month before the end of his second year to say he was thinking of packing it in at the end of the season. He didn't feel he could contribute in the way he wanted to. Before the final game of the 1973/74 season, at home to Rotherham, I called him into the office and said, 'David, this is your last game tomorrow. I want you to leave this club the way you came into it, so people can say it was worth paying good money to see you play.' He didn't let the supporters down, as he was absolutely outstanding. He didn't need me to say it for him, but I felt it was important for him to end on a good note.

Tony Morrin

When Davie joined Exeter I played a couple of games with him, then for the third match I was left out. I was playing quite well so was surprised and thought it might be something to do with Davie, as he'd just joined the club. The evening I heard I'd been dropped Davie came round to my house to explain he had nothing to do with the decision and told me he thought I'd been playing well. Davie had played most of his career at the highest level but still put himself out to see me and I thought that was a magnificent gesture he didn't have to do. That's the nature of the fella and ever since then we've been friends. I thought the world of John Newman as he did well for me and funnily enough that season I didn't miss another game!

Appendix 2

David Gibson Chronology

1938	Born.
1954	Signed for Livingston United. 156 matches, winning the Scottish Juvenile Cup.
1956	Signed for Hibernian.
1959	Selected for Scotland 'A' trial match at Ibrox.
1960	Called up for National Service.
1962	Toured Far East with British Army football team. Transferred to Leicester City for £25,000. 53 goals in 339 games.
1963	FA Cup final *v*. Manchester United. First Scottish cap *v*. Austria.
1963–64	Six Scotland caps *v*. Norway, Republic of Ireland, Spain, Wales, Finland and Northern Ireland.
1964	League Cup final victory *v*. Stoke City.
1965	League Cup final *v*. Chelsea.
1969	FA Cup final *v*. Manchester City.
1970	Transferred to Aston Villa. 24 games, 1 goal.
1971	League Cup final *v*. Tottenham Hotspur.
1972	Transferred to Exeter City. 3 goals in 71 appearances.
1974	Retired.